KING OF THE UNDIES WORLD

Chris Page

psipook press
www.psipook.com

Published by Psipook Press
Copyright©Chris Page
All rights reserved

Chris Page has asserted his right to be identified as the author of this work

First published in 2014 by Psipook Press
This paperback edition, 2014 by Psipook Press
www.psipook.com
psipook@psipook.com

ISBN 978-0-9559588-6-1

The characters and events in this story are all fictitious. Any resemblance to anyone or anything real is as accidental as it is unlikely.

Cover design by Chris Page

For my family

King of the Undies World

Being the first volume in the Underpants of Fire *trilogy*

By Chris Page

Now read on …

1

The effulgently gorgeous and terribly pampered Victoria Gousset has just been kidnapped and is looking forward to a good long hostage drama in the sun.

She is tanning herself on the big stone-flagged terrace of Villa Parque, which is perched elegantly on a clifftop overlooking the Mediterranean. From her sun lounger, she can see the manly cliffs across the bay rising from the frothing ocean to the thrusting peaks above, which are dotted with more luxury villas and quaint villages than she can count. She can count to six on a good day. She is wearing a bikini that is noticeable for its lack of size and substance. Seagulls hover on the ocean breezes to ogle her, clouds peer over the shoulders of the birds to get a better look; above them spy satellites and an alien spaceship jostle for the best view of this young lady resplendent in her beauty.

At Victoria's side is a cocktail of vibrant plumage, which, in confirmation of her absolute luxury, is topped with a paper umbrella.

The sun blesses her, a cool breeze caresses her and fortune grins idiotically upon her. Everything is good.

Sigh.

'Brilliant, isn't it, Timmy.'

Timmy is the Greek god on the same terrace, the one with burnished bronze skin, blazing blond hair, incandescent teeth, and leopard-print trunks that are even smaller than Victoria's bikini. Timmy is currently toning his muscles by lifting a complete set of train wheels.

'What's brilliant, Victoria?'

'The sun, the scenery, the luxury, the indulgence; the sheer, gorgeous gorgeousness of this place.'

Timmy furrowed his brow a moment. 'Yeah, but what's brilliant? What does the word, like, mean? I've heard it before, but haven't figured it out.'

Sigh.

'Brilliant. Like you, Timothy. Don't dwell on it, it'll come to you eventually.'

Timothy Adonis, Victoria's personal assistant, is employed at dramatic expense to do for Victoria; to do all the things Victoria was too rich to do, like make and take telephone calls, pick clothes off the floor, make tea, spread jam on toast, plump sofa cushions and pillows, frown uncomprehendingly at uncomplicated ideas, handle the boring practicalities of whatever, whatever, but mainly just do for Victoria.

He was handpicked by Victoria herself after an exhaustive and exhausting process of phoning a local talent agency and scrutinising processions of the talent they had in stock. He hadn't so far, in six months of employment, shown much aptitude for or understanding of any of the assigned tasks, and especially not *doing* for Victoria. He was, however, very, very good at frowning uncomprehendingly, which he did diligently and absolutely all the time. And he was glowingly, ridiculously gorgeous.

'Oh, put that bloody train down and come and have a glass of steroids.'

'Thank you very much, Victoria. Don't mind if I do.'

'Don't you think it was terribly, terribly clever of me to kidnap myself? Not many people would have thought to do that, you know.'

'Yes,' said Timothy, struggling to keep up with the conversation.

'Well. All this gorgeousness and cleverness comes at a price. I must write a ransom letter to my father to free myself. Don't you think it just delicious irony that I'm writing a ransom letter to my own father to get him to pay money to free me from a kidnapping I've done to myself?'

'Delicious? Yes, the drink is very nice, thank you. Could do with a few more umbrellas, but very nice all the same.'

Victoria opened up the pink laptop that perched on her pretty thighs.

'Dear, Daddy,' she began and paused thoughtfully. 'Timmy. I've been designing lingerie again and I've had some of the designs made up. Let me show them to you later. I'll model them myself.'

'I'm sure they're very nice, Victoria, but I'm afraid I don't know much about lingerie. I only wear leopard-print trunks myself.'

'Dear Daddy, I've just kidnapped your daughter …' she typed.

'Victoria, may I be so bold?'

'Oh, you may be as bold as you like. In fact, you are positively under positive orders to be as positively bold as you like.' She put the laptop aside and wiggled in anticipation in what there was of her bikini.

'Well, it seems to me that if you are kidnapped and your father pays a ransom and then you go home with all the ransom money, isn't your father going to be a tiny bit — you know? Won't he notice?'

'Oh no, not at all. He'll just be glad to see me, number one, and number two, there's so much money sloshing around he won't miss the odd billion here or there. He probably loses track of it himself. We once lost the entire economy of Estonia down the back of the sofa.'

'Didn't she miss it?'
'Who?'
'Estonia.'
'Miss what? The sofa?'

'Miss her economy.'

'Oh. I didn't think to ask. Anyway, as I remember, I found it and spent the whole lot on crisps.'

So much for Timmy's boldness. Victoria went back to her computer.

'May I be bold again, Victoria?'

'I should be so lucky.'

'Why have you kidnapped yourself? After all, a lady of such privilege and fortune cannot lack for anything.'

'I have explained this to you before, Timmy. I explained this before we came here. Then I think I explained it to you on the plane. Then when we got off the plane, and just about every five minutes since then.'

'I thought you might have done. And I think it might be a wee bit difficult.'

'Are you asking me to explain it to you again?'

'Yes, Victoria, I believe I am.'

'And if I explain it again and again and again, will you eventually get the hang of it?'

'I doubt it, Victoria.'

'Oh. OK.'

Sigh.

She put down the computer again.

'Well. Why have I kidnapped myself? Oh, pure spoiled venality I suppose. By venality I mean greed, not the embarrassing social disease.'

'You're welcome.'

'I've lost oodles and oodles of my pocket money gambling. I bet Atlantic City on Las Vegas and it came up Cayman Islands so that was that. Oh, and I wanted a fast car, a unicorn, a spaceship, attention, an exciting life, another unicorn, a new bicycle, the moon, a white elephant, electroshock therapy, fame, love, and a nice holiday away from the pressures of being rich. And above all, I want something else, but I can't think what it is. Oh, yes. Above all I want oodles and oodles of validation. That's what I really want.'

Sigh.

'I told Daddy I wanted a Disney castle and you know

WHO IS THE AUTHOR? WHO IS HE REALLY?

Chris Page was born in Sweden in 1962, and brought up in Gloucestershire in the UK. After living in London and New York, he moved to Osaka in 1989, where he is based to this day with his family.

He is an occasional magazine editor, cartoonist, journalist, and copywriter, and supports all these occupations by working in education. Primarily, he writes fiction and dotes on his big, fat, black and white cat.

In July 2002 *The London Magazine* featured his short story, 'The Freebie'. That story is included alongside more of his short fiction in the e-book collection *Shorts* and paperback *Un-Tall Tales*, also available from Psipook Press. Chris's first novel is *Weed*, also from Psipook Press.

King of the Undies World is the first volume of the *Underpants of Fire* trilogy.

what he said to me?'

'What's Disney?'

'No, silly! He said the most awful thing.'

'The most awful thing? That is awful. How could he say that?'

'He said "Yes."'

'No!'

'Yah! He said "Yes", just like that.'

'What did he do that for?'

'Well, absolutely! Just "Yes" without a thought. I don't suppose he was even listening. So then I said I wanted a Disney prince to go with the Disney castle and he said "Yes" again, so that clinched it. He doesn't care about me. He would rather give me everything and then have me go away with a fictional character rather than actually say he loves me, so that's that. I'm going to teach him a lesson and then take a whole planet worth of money, which I'll spend on the Cayman islands, a Disney castle, a fast car, a unicorn, a spaceship, attention, an exciting life, another unicorn, a new bicycle, the moon, a white elephant, electroshock therapy, fame, love, and a nice holiday away from the pressures of being rich, and the other thing I want above all else, which I can't put a name to right now. Oh, yes. Above all I want oodles and oodles of validation. That's what I'll spend it on.'

'Aren't you having a nice holiday away from the pressures of being rich right now?'

'Well this is gorgeous, isn't it. But this is a kidnap so isn't it a bit like work? I don't know what work's like but I suppose it to be a bit like this.'

She went back to composing the ransom note.

'Dear Daddy, I've just kidnapped your daughter and I'm going to cut myself — her — into small pieces and mail the bits to you one at a time until I receive one million squillion pounds in your daughter's bank account by sundowner time Tuesday.

'I don't know what it is, Timmy, but something is not convincing me about this note.'

'Perhaps you should say what you'll use to cut yourself

into small pieces to show you have thought about this seriously.'

'Good idea! What does one use to cut me into small pieces?'

'I don't know. I've never tried to cut you into small pieces. How about a knife and fork?'

'Hmmm. Dear Daddy, I've just kidnapped your daughter and I'm going to cut herself into small pieces using a chef.'

'You know, it still doesn't sound right. Perhaps I should change the Daddy bit. In business don't people use names like "sir" or "madam"?'

'How about Sir-Madam?'

'Timmy, what's my father's name?'

'Who's your father?'

'Daddy's my father.'

'Is he? Then, his name is Sir Hades Gousset.'

'Is it? He has the same last name as me. That's tidy, I suppose. And "Sir", so that's another hint, I suppose.'

She tapped momentarily on the keyboard. 'Oh bother, writing ransom notes is such hard work. I suppose that's why there aren't more of them. I'm exhausted already. All this finger tapping.'

'Why don't you record your message?'

'What a good idea! A recording! How terribly dramatic too! We can use an orchestra and perhaps we can get the mp3 file to smoke and explode after Daddy has listened to it.'

'That doesn't sound impossible.'

'Here we go. Dear Daddy Sir Hades Gousset, I have kidnapped your daughter, Victoria, and she is going to cut me into small chef-sized bits and send them on a nice holiday in Disneyland.

'Oh, dear, Timmy. That doesn't sound very convincing again, does it. What can be wrong?'

'Perhaps it's the fact that you are addressing your father as your father and he is sure to recognise your voice. These details are likely to undermine the authenticity of the project.'

'Timmy! You said "authenticity"! What's got into you?'

They both looked dubiously at Timmy's glass of steroids.

'Do you think I ought to use more paper umbrellas next time?'

2

Sir Hades Gousset was in his lab testing underwear.

Sir Hades is one of the richest, most successful businessmen on the planet. Sir Hades Gousset is an underpants magnate. Sir Hades Gousset is big in underwear. In fact, he is the biggest magnate in underwear in the world. Compared to Sir Hades, there are just no other big men in underpants — none to touch him, anyway. In fact, Sir Hades Gousset is so big in underpants he is quite simply the biggest man in the world in anything.

Hades Gousset: King of the Undies World!

He who controls underpants controls the world. That's what Sir Hades likes to say.

'What is it every person needs?' he demands at official functions, on TV, at international conferences, at Davos every year, at the speaker's podium in the United Nations, speaker's corner, at dinner, and whenever, wherever he thinks he has an audience.

'Food. Water. Shelter. Underpants. Without these basics, we can do nothing. Food and water mean nourishment and sustaining the body from within. Shelter means safety and security and sustaining the body from without. You may think shelter means the four walls that enclose us when we sleep but that's just part of the story. We have a more fundamental sense of shelter and it's usually to be found in our trousers. A shelter most basic; essential shelter. Because even when we are in our walled space, our cave, or wherever we feel safe, we crave security at a more intimate level: the cosseting shelter only our undergarments can provide.

'Underpants separate us from the animals. Our foundation wear is the base on which civilisation is built. Why, I once lived with a tribe of nomads who were underpants averse. Did they have civilisation? Did they build bridges or tall buildings or aeroplanes or free market economies? No, they had caravans and bad hair and were arrested by the police.

'You could say — and I do say — no pants, no life!'

And so it was that Sir Hades saw himself as providing an essential humanitarian service, extending civilisation to all loins that craved it, while earning huge pots of dosh in the process. His underpants brand and retail chain, Hades Undies World, were in every department store, on every high street, in every mall, on everyone's lips and in everyone's trousers. The company's flaming underpants logo was the most recognised trademark on the planet. Meanwhile, Hades' corporate interests, research and development division was taken care of by his parent company, Pants Corp.

'I thought to myself a long time ago, that if you can provide the basics to people at an affordable price, you can be a very rich person while spreading the benefits of sophisticated culture.'

And his philosophy had amassed him a wealth bigger than the Himalayas.

'This way, Sir Hades. The tests are about to begin.' Dr Edwin Pickles, in white lab coat and saucer-like spectacles, directed Sir Hades to his sandbagged observation point within the vast hanger that was the site for the physical tests here at the facility formerly known as Porton Down, the famous top secret research centre, which Sir Hades has bought off a cash-strapped government thus saving the UK from economic ruin — again. On purchasing the Porton Down complex, Hades renamed it to fit in with his empire. Porton Down became Pants Down. Anyone who had dealings with, or passing knowledge of the place, liked to use its original name.

Addressing the collection of technicians in the bunker, Sir Hades declaimed, 'Ladies and gentlemen. We are making underwear history. We are no longer just providing the traditional function of underwear, which is shelter and catching drips. We are now on a mission to extend that concept of shelter to its logical consequence. We are about to introduce underpants and their wearers to the notions of protection, safety and rescue.'

There was really no need for Sir Hades to announce this to his technicians. They already knew. More than that, they had the task of taking Sir Hades' dreams and making them a working reality. They had the task, as do workers everywhere, of doing the real work while the boss sat back and chewed cigars and thought up ever more delusional projects. But they were being paid oodles, so whatever.

'Who's up first, Pickles?'

'The first test pilot is Felix Baumkuchen. He's testing the flying underpants.'

'Excellent. Make sure there's a tot of brandy for the chap when he lands.'

'Already taken care of, sir,' beamed Pickles. His smile disconcertingly magnified by his saucer spectacles.

'Flying underpants. Fantastic things! Imagine: you're in the path of a runaway lorry: leap into the air and your underpants will fly you out of harm's way. You find yourself on top of a suddenly erupting volcano: jump into the air and your underpants will whisk you to safety. On the Alpine slopes, suddenly there's an enormous avalanche: gather your fellows in your arms, jump into the sky and fly them all to the chalet for a hot gluhwein.'

Sir Hades looked up into the steel spars of the ceiling through his binoculars and found Felix Baumkuchen on a high gantry and wearing nothing but a flying helmet, goggles and an enormous pair of grey Y-fronts.

Like Sir Hades far below, he was surrounded by busy technicians bearing tablets and wearing flash goggles.

'Look, here, Pickles, the wings on the pants are already deployed but the fellow hasn't left the gantry yet.'

'That's right. Since this is the maiden flight, we thought we'd test the aerodynamics of the wings first for safety reasons.'

'Say what, Mr Man? Nonsense! Perfectly safe. Launch with the wings in stowed position, because that's the way they would normally be in an emergency. Deploy in the air, the way it will happen in a real emergency.'

'Oh, do you really think that's wise, Sir Hades? What if …'

'I'm looking through these incredibly powerful binoculars and, you know, I don't see any whats or ifs or buts anywhere. Stow those wings, like a good chap, eh?'

Pickles gave the order.

'Are we ready now?' he asked Sir Hades.

'Yes, we jolly well are.'

'Handing the comm to mission control,' said Dr Pickles into the tiny mic attached to his ear.

'Mission control acknowledging command of the comm,' said the earnest crew-cut man standing next to him into his own tiny mic. 'Commencing countdown. Three, two, one, Geronimo!'

Felix Baumkuchen leapt into the void, arms outstretched before him in the universal posture of flying without an aeroplane, and soared gracefully. The appearance of graceful soaring was an optical illusion brought on by holding your breath in anticipation of finding out whether you've earned a big fat bonus for a job well done, or a week in the janitor's shed with the cans of solvent for a job not well done. In reality, gravity was just getting a firm grip on Felix Baumkuchen before yanking him to the concrete floor a hundred metres below and depositing him there with a loud splat, and where the wings at last deployed.

'Bugger. Back to the drawing board with that one,' said Sir Hades.

The technicians exchanged alarmed looks, mouthed 'Drawing board! We forgot the drawing board!' at each other and made hurried notes on their tablets.

'What about the brandy,' asked Dr Pickles.

'Hardy Perfection. One hundred and forty years. Cognac. Too good to waste. Pour it on him. I'm sure some will percolate in through the holes.

'Who's next?'

'Next we have Buzz Adrenalin. He's testing the parachuting underpants.'

'Fantastic. The parachuting underpants. We all need those. Trapped at the pinnacle of a flaming skyscraper: simply leap to safety. In a doomed aeroplane plummeting to certain death: jump out the window with an armful of women and children and lower everyone to the ground. How about the suicide, tired of life? Decides to end it all by throwing himself off Lover's Leap — but then halfway down he gets a text from his beloved begging reconciliation. Suddenly life is worth living again. He only need thrust his hand in his trousers and float to a happy ending. Let's see these bloomers bloom!'

Sir Hades and all the technicians once again focused their binoculars on the gantry, mission control went through the launch protocols — 'Geronimo!' — and again gravity did what gravity does best.

'Brandy, sir?'

'As before, Pickles. And one for me. Next?'

'Next, sir, Flash Boredom.'

'The bouncing underpants. Brilliant! Think of the mountaineer slipping from the embrace of his ropes and tumbling the sheer wall from a towering peak. He can simply inflate his underwear and bounce to the bottom. Caught on a level crossing with your foot jammed in the rail and a massive goods train barreling down on you? Inflate those pants to cushion the blow. Erm, erm, changing light bulbs on the rickety stepladder, a potentially bone snapping tumble will turn into a humorous bounce. Erm, erm ...' Sir Hades was running out of inspiration.

'Our initial tests have shown that children can use inflated bouncing underpants as substitute space hoppers and thereby hours of innocent playground fun.'

'Missing the point a bit,' growled the mogul. 'Underpants are supposed to be functional, not fun. I suppose we could re-brand the playground pants at a push. Let's get on with it. I've a good feeling about these bouncers.'

The test pilot Flash Boredom seemed a bit reluctant to launch but a helpful prod from a flight technician with a broom soon had him airborne and straightaway after that, the cleaning staff had more mopping up to do.

'Let's switch brandy, eh. That Spanish stuff, Orina de Bull, we picked up in Torremolinos, the stuff we use for cleaning the silver, will do. I'll stick with the Perfection, though.'

3

Sir Hades was thoughtful. 'Interesting test results this morning. I believe we're on to something here. I say we combine the flight function, the parachute function and the bounce function in one set of underpants. It'll be a mega seller. What do you say, Pickles? Good man! Get on it!'

Ms Hilda Titanium, personal assistant to Sir Hades, strode into the bunker carrying a large brown, padded envelope. Her presence instantly electrified the room. Eyewear steamed up. Eyes without wear steamed up.

Hilda Titanium was not just a personal assistant, she made the world go round. She made men's heads spin. She was a force of nature; a force of nature in a sackcloth dress. The sackcloth dress was a health and safety precaution: if she were clad in any normal dress, men's heads would spin off completely.

'Sir Hades, sir. I have an urgent communication for you.'

'Can't it wait? We're about to test the shark-repelling underpants. I'm looking forward to that. Important work, you know.'

'You need to see this, sir.'

'Oh, buggery bugger-bags!'

'If you'll excuse us,' Hilda told the personnel in the bunker who fled for the door as one, clenching their teeth and clutching themselves.

'Sir, this was delivered a short while ago, addressed to you. As with all your mail, I took the liberty of opening it. There's a note ... and something else.'

Sir Hades read the note: "Sir Hades Gousset, esq., I hope you are well. Your daughter Victoria Gousset has been kidnapped. I enclose a thumb. Yours sincerely faithfully sincerely, the Kidnapper."

'What? What? Victoria's thumb? Who did this? What bastard barbarian has kidnapped my daughter and sent me her thumb? When I catch up with him, I'll cut off more than his thumb —'

'Sir Hades, thumb as in drive, not thumb as in opposable. Thumb as in USB digital storage device, not thumb as in pollex.' Hilda held up the memory stick. It was an expensive model, nauseatingly pink and suffering a rash of sequins.

'There's an audio file on it. I rather suspect it will turn out to be a message of some sort pertaining to the abduction. A plea from Victoria, perhaps; proof that they have her and she is alive. It may contain ransom demands.'

'When I catch up with the bastard who did this, I'll cut off his pollices and feed them to him at great speed. Let's listen to this damn recording then.'

Hilda plugged the drive into a lab laptop and opened the audio file.

The recording was of a female voice doing a bad impersonation of a man with a Germanic accent.

'Hairy Sir Hades Gousset, guten morning —' giggle 'Ve haff your daughter, Victoria Gousset. If you do not cooperate viz all our demands, ve vill cut her into small pieces, ja, and feed her to herself —' suppressed laughter — 'vizout seasoning.' More suppressed laughter. 'Ze only vay to save her is to pay a squillion million spondulicks into a numbered Swiss bank account, which will be in Switzerland, and which will have a number. The number is on the accompanying note.'

Sir Hades scrutinised the paper in his hand but could see no number on either side.

'You have until sundowner time tomorrow to comply or

Victoria is sashimi. Woo ha ha ha ha!' The recording closed with suppressed laughter.

At that moment, Hilda's own personal assistant appeared in the bunker. 'Ms Titanium, I'm terribly sorry to interrupt, but we have another package just like the first. I thought you'd like to see it right away.'

'Thank you, Catshit.' The package, which was indeed a plain, padded envelope like the original contained a note on a single sheet of paper.

"Hi. Sorry. Forgot to attach this with the first note," it read.

And there followed a long number which apparently referred to an account at the Swiss Cottage, London, branch of Big Bank PLC.

With a fizz and a pop, the pink thumb drive went up in smoke and vapour.

'Good Lord,' exclaimed Sir Hades. 'I didn't know they could make an MP3 file do that.'

'I don't think they can, Sir Hades. I suspect the computer's logic board has been contaminated with the chemicals you were using in the shark repelling underpants.'

4

Sir Hades stared at the now silent computer and then at the notes in his hand.

'My daughter. My one and only daughter. Snatched by unspeakable villains. Stolen from the bosom of her family by evil, twisted minds. Her life threatened and used as a means of extorting honestly earned money from her doting father. Rapacious, callous, evil monsters clutching my pure and beautiful daughter.

'My arse!

'That was Victoria herself, wasn't it.'

'I'm afraid it was, Sir Hades,' confirmed Hilda.

'I'd know that crap German accent anywhere, and that imbecilic giggle she gets after a couple of cocktails. What the hell is she playing at? Do we have any idea where she is?'

'Not at the moment. I'll send the envelopes and note over to the forensic labs right away and let the white coats give them a good sniff.'

'Now, where's her wosserfeller, that dozy Neanderthal, her assistant. Timpani Twonk, or whatever. Perhaps he can shed some light on this nonsense.'

'Perhaps you mean Timothy Adonis. Catshit, can you track down Mr Adonis, for me?'

'Yes, with due servility, Ms Titanium.' Catshit tugged a forelock he carried around for the purpose and retreated into a corner of the room with his smart phone.

'Good grief, Hilda. What has got into the girl?'

'Oh, mindless greed, I would say, Sir Hades. And a degree of sociopathy that enables her to extort from her own father.'

'Haven't I always provided for her? Haven't I given her everything she needed? Just the other day, she asked for a Disney castle, and I said yes. Which do you want? Tokyo, Paris, Florida or California? Shall I commission Mickey to make one for you himself? I understand he has dwarves just for that sort of thing.

'She's never been without undergarments, you know. They call undergarments foundation wear because they are the foundation of everything. No undergarments, no life. And she has had the best, the most snug, the woolliest underthings a father can provide.'

'I know, dear Sir Hades, I know.'

Catshit scuttled out of his corner.

'It is with utmost cringing that I interrupt again,' he began.

'Have you found Timothy?'

'Yes, sir and milady. And I believe I have found Miss Victoria, too.'

'Say what, Mr Man? You found my daughter in the short time it took me to get through that dreary, time-filling exposition in which I was compelled to sound self-pitying even though I'm not like that at all?'

'Yes, your exultancy.'

'Catshit!'

'Take a rise, Catshit!'

'Oh thank you, sir. Which rise shall I take?'

'Primrose Hill! Yes, take Primrose Hill. That's a very nice rise.'

'Thank you, Sir Hades, sir.'

'But you still have to work both Christmas Eve and Boxing Day, Catshit,' said Hilda. 'And I'm going to begrudge you the salary I pay you for Christmas Day even though you won't be working.'

'I appreciate it, Ms Titanium. It shows you care.'

'Right. Catshit. What have you got for us?'

'Well, I couldn't get Timmy at his office or on his mobile or at home, so I called his family. They said he was assisting Miss Victoria kidnap herself and they gave me the address he gave them in case of emergencies.' Reading from a note: 'Villa Parque, In the Sun, South of France.'

'Will you be going in person, Sir Hades? Should I inform your wife? Would you like me to go on your behalf? Shall I summon the highly paid ex-special forces mercenaries you keep for unconventional jobs?'

'None of the above, Hilda, dear. I want to think on this a moment.'

5

Sir Hades Gousset is now the most important man on the planet. Almost all the residents of planet earth have entrusted their most intimate zones to his hands, so to speak. However, Sir Hades has not always been so exulted. What he has, whatever heights he has reached have been achieved by himself and himself alone. There was no leg up with a family fortune — he had no family. There was no old boy network from his school or college unless you needed needed a janitor or someone to empty a septic tank. Sir Hades, you see, came from the most humble beginnings imaginable. He was born in a ditch. In Essex, at that.

It is right and proper to point out at this point that ditches are neither a characteristic nor quality of Essex. Nor did his mother in her labour plod for hours around the county looking for a ditch in which to give birth. Nor was Hades' mother thinking particularly about giving Hades humble beginnings. She wasn't even thinking about giving birth. She was thinking, as she stumbled into the one and only ditch in Essex, about protecting her bottle of gin so that it didn't get broken.

The bottle of gin survived long enough to be consumed by the mother of the infant Hades, who was born right there without his mother noticing or even remembering that she was with child.

When the bottle was empty and when Hades' mother eventually regained consciousness, the woman climbed out of the ditch and was gone, and that was that for Hades' mother's involvement in her child's upbringing.

At first, Hades was raised by the rats of the ditch. When cats took an interest in the rats and the rats moved involuntarily up to the next rung of the food chain — or up into the inhabitants of the next rung of the food chain — the cats took over nursing the infant man-child and taught him to stop twitching his whiskers in such a vulgar, rodent-like manner. Dogs — Essex dogs, presumably — eventually moved in and the cats upped and went in search of less animated objects to stare at. The dogs quickly taught Hades that there was no need for him to spend so much time licking his shoulders or hands when there were other parts of his anatomy he could lick with more obvious reward.

The dogs attracted humans: nomads of the music festival, road building and caravan park culture who taught him how to creatively style his hair using only mud to hold its shape.

Hades could not say he was happy. All Hades could say was "squeak", "miaow", and "woof."

The nomads attracted the attention of the police, social services, Range Rover-driving landowners and animal protection agencies, who found a totally naked Hades running around with the nomads' dogs. Hades became the object of a brief legal tussle between all the four interested parties. The social services and animal protection agencies each claimed they ought to take him into care. The social services argued that as a human-child, Hades was obviously their responsibility. The animal welfare people argued that he ought to be in a home for abused animals if not an actual zoo for careful study as a potentially new species. The police wanted to arrest him for his hairstyle and the Range Rover driving landowners thought he'd be good for target practice, or something for their hounds to practice on.

In the end DNA tests proved, quite improbably, that the

young Hades thing was indeed human and so social services took over.

They placed him in a residence for orphans and abandoned children. The first thing that happened when he got there was a shower. Then a bath. Then another shower and a lot more dunking in the bath and vigorous scrubbing while the staff tried to find the child entombed in the dirt.

It was then that the transformative and defining event of Hades' life occurred: the staff of the social services gave him, for the first time since exiting his mother's womb in the Essex ditch, clothes. On top of the pile of new soft, clothes things was a pair of white, utilitarian, Y-fronts and it was these he tried on first. He had never experienced anything so clean and snug and reassuring. Hades stood in the middle of his small, bare socially-serviced room and stared down at the cotton that was comforting and protecting his loins.

There was no mirror in the room. There was no mirror in the room because some residents were inclined to smash them and then use the shards of glass to slash themselves or other people. So Hades simply stared at himself in the vague reflection in the bottom of his tin cup. Covered and tucked up thus he discovered security and belonging. He felt safe. Complete. He now no longer looked like an animal. He looked human. He was grateful to the rats and the cats and the dogs and the nomads for bringing him this far, but it was as if deep down he had always known he was different. The animals of course had no need for undies. They had fur and were all id. They hadn't thought that the man-child might need anything around his loins — other than a tongue from the point of view of the dogs. And the nomads, although dressed, eschewed underwear on the grounds that it needed washing and changing, and, even worse, needed buying or stealing and they had a whole bunch of more pressing things to be not bothering with.

Hades now understood he was destined to wear underpants. His life started making sense to him — sense where before the possibility of sense had been an entirely absent concept, like family, love, Sunday roasts or quantum physics.

He put on the rest of the clothes and looked like a person at last. He walked the corridors of the orphanage with confidence and a new resolve in his step and admired himself in every reflective surface he could find. No matter how good he looked in his institutional sweats, it was what was underneath them that made him feel real.

It was at this home that another life-shaping experience occurred.

Just as the rats of Hades' ditch attracted the cats, which attracted the dogs, which attracted the nomads, this institution full of young, vulnerable people attracted the kind of people who had uses for young vulnerable people. These individuals came from outside the orphanage but had ways of insinuating themselves within the community. Hades, as a new young and freshly scrubbed young thing with no particular command of human language to tell tales was of especial interest. One day, a visitor managed to engineer, on some pretext or other, an hour or two alone with Hades. The visitor's cries alerted the staff, who had him rushed to hospital where he had his own fingers surgically removed from his own orifices.

Hades got into no trouble. Quite the opposite. He was awarded new, whiter, snugger underpants.

And so Hades made good progress at the orphanage. He was respected and did well in his classes.

There was only one spot of crap in the ointment. Coming to them with no history and no family, the staff were obliged to choose a name on behalf of the young Hades, and so they did.

But to choose a name? Well, traditionally, names reflected something about the bearer, their origin, their place in society, their qualities. Crazy Horse, named for the strength and virility of the noble equine; Carpenter, named for the practical skill of the artisan; Wood, dweller among trees; Page, a lowly lackey or a flunky, something to be dressed up and then kicked about by beings higher up the social pile; Bakewell, being from the place where the tarts were made; Squire, a manner of conception. The staff might have named Hades Born-In-A-Ditch-Of-A-Woman-Who-Was-Too-Pissed-To-Notice-She-Was-Even-Pregnant but that part of Hades' history was unknown and so he was dubbed Feral-Unwanted-And-Abandoned-Foundling. Marlon Feral-Unwanted-And-Abandoned-Foundling.

Right away, Hades hated the name Marlon. It was affected. It was excruciatingly embarrassing being named after a film star.

And so the bullying began. The kids at the orphanage taunted him over being called Marlon. Shopkeepers, bus drivers, strangers, giggled when the heard his name. School registrars and post office workers guffawed. Eventually even the social services officials who had named him couldn't help but join in the mocking.

However, Marlon, who had endured ditches and rats and cats and dogs and nomads and molesters was not going to passively accept this ridicule. He was after all, a wearer of underpants — clean underpants. The underpants gave him faith, and certainty and confidence; they gave him destiny; and it was through his robust, underthings-inspired responses to the teasing that a new name was born: Hades; the fiery one.

Under the fire he rained down, the taunting stopped, and in time the bruises healed.

Meanwhile, Hades excelled at school and quickly revealed a talent for all things scientific: maths, chemistry, physics, biology, and digesting institutional food. When these merged into an interest in fabrics and tolerances of various kinds of elastic, his fate and future were sealed.

And so it was to university and the beginning of the most spectacular career in anything the planet had ever seen.

A new start in life was as good as any time to get a new name. He would leave behind the ditch and the stigma of Marlon. He changed his name to Hades, and then, because he could, and because people had a problem spelling Feral-Unwanted-And-Abandoned-Foundling, he adopted a new surname too: Gousset, because gousset meant gusset, which best represented his vocation; and gousset was French, and the musicality and sophistication of a foreign language evoked a lofty ideal where plain old gusset evoked a creepy obsession.

And the rest, as they say, is to be explained on a later page.

And what of the ditch? It was eventually removed to a county — name withheld for legal reasons — with which it was more in character, its role in history, in the making of one of the most extraordinary characters in the annals of human stuff and wotsit, unknown to anyone but the readers of this history.

6

It is a beautiful evening at Villa Parque. It is a beautiful everything at Villa Parque. The moon is full and glorious and opalescent. A warm breeze carries the scent of bougainvillea and appalling wealth.

Timothy is juggling ancient stone statues. Life-size depictions of classical gods and fantastic young ladies in togas. He is practicing so that he can amuse Victoria with the trick later.

He is sure that Victoria wants nothing more than to see him juggling mock-ancient stone statues.

Victoria emerges from the villa and on to the terrace. She is wearing a diaphanous negligee and flimsy, silky things. She stops and poses, hand on hip, in Timothy's line of sight.

'Hello,' said Timothy. 'Do you want to see me juggle? I was doing it with five statues before, but I accidentally tossed one in the ocean.'

'Timmy. I told you before that I had been designing lingerie. Things my father has no interest in making. Well, this is one of my creations.'

Without taking his eyes off the spinning statues, Timothy said, 'Nice colour. Suits you.'

'There's more in the collection. I'll show you another.'

She went back inside the villa for a moment and emerged in another outfit. This time there was no negligee, but there was a lot of lace and frilly stuff and borderline transparency.

'What do you think?'

'Er. I'm not really a judge of fashion. My parents didn't really wear lingerie. They wear clothes and wardrobes and stuff. Nice colour, though. Suits you.'

'My father doesn't like this stuff. He won't let me manufacture it. We don't agree on anything.

'He just thinks underwear is about being sensible. That's all he's interested in, sensible underwear. Snug and warm and sensible and boring. You see, I always thought underwear was about sex. Sex, Timmy. I thought it was about softness and silkiness and sensuality and love and romantic things. And of course about catching drips but mostly about sex. But Daddy doesn't see it like that at all. All he cares about is practicalities and money and owning things and owning people.

'I'll try on another set. No, it's OK. There's no need for me to go inside. I'll change right here. I don't mind. We're all adults.'

She stepped out of her frilly, lacy things and stepped into others that were even frillier and lacier and more transparent and much, much smaller.

'Oh, Timmy, don't you just love sensuality and romance?'

'I love juggling.'

'Oh, Timmy, I love ...'

'I'm not much of a romantic, but my colleague is drooling all over himself. Lady, in terms of giving hints, you need a sledgehammer to get through to your man friend.'

Timothy lost control of the statues he was juggling which sailed in a beautifully orderly line over the parapet of the terrace and down to the ocean below.

Just behind Victoria two dark figures had emerged from the Villa. The moonlight, which one moment had seemed romantic and serene, now seemed sinister and tainted. Each of the newcomers carried evil-looking guns. The one who had spoken, the taller of the two, had a woman's voice but wore a black ski mask. The one at her side was shorter and was also wearing a ski mask. Drool was indeed escaping, copiously, from the mouth hole.

The woman spoke. 'Big man, don't make a move. We're not here for you, so if you behave you can get back to tossing your cabers or whatever it was you were doing. We're here for the little lady. Get in the bag little lady.'

The speaker tossed a large overnight bag at Victoria's feet.

'You leave her —'

'Stay where you are big man. You may look like Atlas himself, but I don't think you'd stand up to a boo, would you.'

'I said, leave her —'

'Boo!'

Timothy screamed and leapt back in terror. He tripped on the balustrade of the terrace and plunged out of sight.

'See,' said the masked figure.

Victoria ran to the edge of the terrace and looked down but all she could see was the implacable waves slooshing around whitely on the black rocks below.

'Timmy! Timmy!' Turning to the intruders: 'You've killed Timmy, you bastards!'

'All part of the service, lady. Now get in the bag.'

'You're horrible and I'm not getting in your rotten bag.'

'Your time has come, Maul. Put her in the bag.'

The shorter of the two said nothing and did nothing. More drool escaped from the mouth hole of the ski mask and contributed to the large pool already around the drooler's feet.

'Maul, I said put her in the bag.' No response; more drool.

'Maul!' The woman kicked Maul in the buttocks.

'What?'

'I said put her in the bag.'

'Oh, were you talking to me? Sorry. Didn't realise.'

Now the hunched figure moved, wading out of the drool pool and squelching across the flagging to Victoria.

'Go away you monster!'

Victoria grabbed the nearest thing, which was her cocktail on the table, and hurled it at Maul. It bounced off his head and made a mess on the stone floor.

She tried hitting him with a chair, which similarly bounced off his head.

The tall woman inspected her fingernails.

Once within arm's reach, Maul simply picked up the furiously kicking and punching Victoria and carried her to the bag, into which he dumped her and zipped her.

'Thank you, Maul. Let's get going.'

'One minute, Davinia,' said Maul. He returned to the terrace table where he finished off Timmy's glass of steroids. 'Waste not, want not.'

'OK, let's go now.'

Maul hauled the wriggling bag on to his shoulder. 'And you don't have to call me Maul, Davinia. It's a bit like me calling you Flay. You can use my first name, you know. My name is Jeremy.'

'Maul. You've left DNA all over the terrace. Very sloppy.'

'Oh for flop's sake.' Maul dumped the bag, which screamed. He got down on all fours and slurped up the drool pool. Standing again, he wiped his mouth on the back of his hand and asked, 'Better now?'

'Most people would have mopped up the drool. But not you.'

'I'm not most people.'

'And thank God for that. If you were most people I would have taken up a career in genocide.'

7

'My daughter kidnapped? But who would do such a thing? Is she OK? Have they harmed her? Have you told the police?'

Persephone was taking the news of her daughter's kidnapping well. She had screamed, run around the room, assaulted a servant with a lamp and upended a Louis XV side table decked with priceless vases.

'We don't know who did it, yes, she seems to be OK, and no, we haven't told the police.'

'Well, we should tell the police immediately.'

Persephone Gousset, Hades' wife, Victoria's mother, was a woman of extravagant proportions, extravagant emotions, and an equally extravagant taste in bling.

'The kidnappers were most explicit about not contacting the police.'

'Who cares what the kidnappers want? Get in touch with the police!'

'I care very much what the kidnappers want. They have our daughter and they did say that if we didn't comply, they would indeed harm her.'

'They would cut her into small pieces and feed her to herself, unseasoned, was the exact threat, I believe, Mrs Gousset,' said Catshit, Hilda Titanium's personal assistant, very solemnly.

Persephone shrieked. 'They threatened what?'

Hilda took charge of her assistant. 'Thank you very much, Catshit. You may now go bury yourself in the garden.'

'Very good, milady.'

'Next to the rhubarb, please. It thrives on fertiliser,' put in Hades.

'I'm on my way, sir.'

'Oh, Hades, and you're just standing there looking at me. Do something!' She hurled a Byzantine figurine through the French window, which was closed.

'Oh, I'm on it. I'm very much on it. Those kidnappers are going to regret tangling with me.' Suppressing a giggle, Sir Hades went on his best business-like way with Hilda Titanium in tow.

8

Hilda Titanium and Sir Hades Gousset walked together through the expansive topiary back towards the main helicopter park of the family home. The topiary was an eerie place to some, but Hades believed that carving bushes to recreate scenes of Hieronymus Bosch's visions of Hell was salutary and morally instructive.

'Did you really need to tell her?' asked Hilda.

'Oh, yes. Imagine: beloved daughter gets back from traumatic kidnapping event and says, hi, Mum, I'm back safe and sound, but it was a horrible ordeal, and Mum says, what was a horrible ordeal? And did your father know about this? There may be more terrible ways to die, but not many, and certainly none louder.'

'How long do you intend to hold Victoria captive?'

'Until she has learned the error of her ways. Kidnapping is not a game, it's a serious crime. People have been killed, lives wrecked in kidnap situations. She obviously needs to become acquainted with reality. And to attempt to extort money from your own father when you already have everything you need ... I would have to spank her soundly if I weren't already scaring seven shades of fear out of her by letting her believe she has been kidnapped for real.'

'And when she has learned her lesson?'

'I'm not a complete monster. I'm on my way down

there now to stage a dramatic rescue. I bound into the kidnappers' den, and bound out again with the distressed damsel and into the glare of publicity. We all come up smelling of roses. I have the boys in the lab working on some new underwear for just such a mission. Could well turn into a new line. Double-oh pants, we might call it. Mission-in-Pants. Special Air Pants. Commando Pants. That sort of thing.'

'I'm sure they'll be very sensible pants.'

'GPS. That's the way to go. Built in GPS system so that you need never get lost. Could link it to a guidance system.'

'Guided pants?'

'Quite so. There are already such things as guided missiles. Why not guided pants? Plug in the GPS coordinates of your target and the smart elastic in the leggings will direct you without any need to look at a map or computer. Your eyes and ears and fighting arms will be free for other tasks. If you insist on going off course, the pants will alert you with a loud klaxon noise.'

'I don't suppose they'd be armour plated too, would they?'

'Crikey! Kevlar. Carbon fibre. Not a problem.'

'They're what every soldier needs.'

'Big market among boy scouts too, I shouldn't wonder.'

'Is this entirely wise, Sir Hades? If I may be so bold as to wonder.'

'GPS in your pants? If there were a short circuit, I suppose you might get a nasty shock but bunging some rubber in the compounds will sort that out.'

'No, I mean faking the kidnapping of your daughter as a response to her faking her own kidnapping.'

'Fighting fire with fire, you know.'

'Well, I mean isn't leaving her with Maul and Flay a bit risky? Maul isn't the most intelligent person on the planet, and Flay isn't the most humane.'

'Maul and Flay? They wouldn't dare bugger with me. They know I'd set Gnash and Grr on them.'

'Quite so. Is there anything I can do?'

'I'll say. You can round up the world's press for me. My underpants will send you the coordinates to gather them once I'm on the move. Talking about fighting fire with fire, have I told you about my idea for flame retardant underpants?'

'Actually, yes, and we manufactured them, if you remember. They had a problem with spontaneous combustion and we had to recall the entire line.'

'I'm talking about different flame retardant underpants. The gimmick with these is that they don't spontaneously catch fire.'

'Now, there's a clever idea.'

9

Persephone Gousset, gouging holes in the 18th century ceiling roses and cornices with an original Queen Anne chair, was tempted to call the police herself. But if, just if, the kidnappers did find out, there's no knowing what they would do to Victoria. Well, she did know what they would do to Victoria, because they had told her through Catshit. They absolutely could not feed Victoria to herself. Her constitution was way too delicate to put up with that.

She would leave the police alone until she had a better idea of what was going on. It was clear that Hades wasn't telling her something and that he had something up his sleeve. You didn't become that big in underpants without not telling people a few things and without having something up your sleeve.

But what was he up to? She had never been in this sort of situation and was not sure how to proceed. Well, exceptional circumstances called for exceptionally odd people.

She needed snoopers to, to, to snoop around. Who were those fixers Hades liked to use? Gnash and Grr? No, too indiscriminately violent. Hades used them when he needed a change in government or a continent shifted over a bit. Maul and Flay? Yes, those are the people he used when he wanted anything creepy done. Now where might she find their number?

Persephone had the servants find her laptop and smartphone in the wreckage of the room and when they were eventually recovered she set about scouring her contacts book. No Mauls or Flays there. She widened the search and eventually tracked them down on Facebook where they had a page. The status report on the page said that Maul and Flay were having a nice time in the south of France where they were holding a kidnap victim hostage. What a coincidence, thought Persephone, they were obviously the right kind of people to talk to and she congratulated herself on her intuition. She liked the page out of courtesy and copied their phone number.

Maul answered the phone.

'What?'

'I'm sorry to bother you. Am I speaking to Maul or Flay?'

'Dunno. Are you?'

'Well, I assume I'm speaking to one of you.'

'Oh yes, there's only one of me. Davinia was quite clear about that.'

Persephone felt she probably had the right number.

'I assume I am speaking to Mr Maul because you don't sound like a Ms Flay.'

'Hold on.' There was some rustling and a ripping sound.

'I just checked my tattoo. Yes, I'm Maul.'

'Excellent. Well, may I then engage you?'

Maul burst into tears. 'That's so beautiful! We've only just met, and electronically at that, and she's proposing to me. Oh, yes! Yes! With all my heart, yes!'

'This is most embarrassing, I'm sure. I didn't mean engage in that sense, I meant in the sense of work. May I engage you to do a job for me? Hire you. Sorry about that.'

The tears ended immediately in one loud nasal slurping suck.

'Oh. Of course. Why would anything nice happen to me? What do you want, then?'

'My daughter has apparently been kidnapped and I'd like you to find out what you can about it. Discreetly.'

'All right. I suppose so. We cost, you know. We ain't friggin' cheap. Nobody,' he said gravely, 'can accuse us of being friggin' cheap'

'That's fine. How much do you charge for a job like this?'

'Whatever we always charge.'

'That'll be fine.'

'So what do you want to know?'

'My name is Persephone Gousset — perhaps you've heard of me.'

'No.'

'And my daughter is Victoria Gousset. She's 22, extremely beautiful and intelligent and she was kidnapped a couple of days ago. And since you and Ms Flay are not unacquainted with the business of kidnapping, I was wondering whether you knew anything.'

'Yes. I know a thing or two.'

'Wonderful.'

Silence.

'Such as ...'

'I know that cats get wet in water and trees don't grow upside down. If you want tomato ketchup from the bottle, take the top off first. It unscrews to either the left or the right. I forget which, so I might on occasion use an axe.'

'I mean, do you know anything about my daughter's kidnapping? I will pay for any information you have and pay a lot if you investigate her disappearance and perhaps find her.'

Sigh. 'Why didn't you say? What do you want to know?'

'Well. I thought you might have heard something.'

'Heard something? Like heard cries for help? Yes, I heard those.'

'My god! Where did you hear them? When?'

'At Villa Parque. When I was putting her in the bag. They don't usually go quietly, you know, though the dead ones tend to be a bit quieter. I personally think it's because they don't like going in the bag. I quite like being in a bag myself so I never understood it, but there you go. Different strokes.'

'You put my daughter in a bag?'

'It's a nice bag, but as I say, she didn't like it. We generally put people in bags when we snatch them. It saves putting up with flailing arms and legs and all that, which get in the way terribly. I take it you ain't never snatched anyone. And bags have carrying straps for carrying, which is handy. People generally don't come with carrying straps, which is a big reason a bag is useful.'

'Well, you release her at once, do you hear? Let her go now!'

'Why? Is there a change of plan? Sir Hades was very clear we shouldn't let her go until he got here.'

'My husband knows where Victoria is?'

'I should say so. It was all his idea. He said that Victoria had been a naughty girl pretending that she had been kidnapped to make unreasonable demands on Walt Disney or something, and that Davinia and I should grab her from Villa Parque to put the righteous fear of kidnapping in her and that he would meet us here and pretend to rescue her and bound into the smell of roses or some such. It all sounded a bit technical to me.'

'My husband kidnapped his own daughter to teach her a lesson about kidnapping?'

'You are your husband's wife, aren't you? I'm surprised you didn't know. It's none of my business, but is there something your husband isn't telling you?'

'You seem like a nice intelligent young man. How would you like to hear a new pro — new business idea?'

10

When Maul emerged from the toilet, Flay noticed the phone in his hand.

'Have you been talking on the telephone again, Maul? You know what I said about talking on the telephone.'

Maul inserted a big grubby finger in his nose and fished out a large, green disgusting thing.

'Oh, yes. But I done good. I think you're going to like this.'

And he popped the big, green disgusting thing into his mouth and chewed with relish.

11

Sir Hades Gousset had a pleasant and leisurely trip to the south of France from England.

His new ninja fighting pants caused some alarms to go off by discharging shuriken in the VIP lounge at Heathrow but he worked around that inconvenience by paying lavish compensation to the victims on the spot.

He whiled away the flight on his private jet by designing travel underwear that would instantly translate any language in the world into your own language and feed you lists to local five-star hotels on demand.

On arriving he made straight for Monte Carlo and the Hôtel de Paris, where he enjoyed a sumptuous feed undisturbed by the ninja pants, which he left twitching in an armoured box in his room.

After that he took a leisurely promenade along the sea front and found diversion in a casino for a few hours. As a moral and upright man, he thoroughly disapproved of gambling except when there was no one around to see him doing it. Finally, he turned in for the night content in the knowledge that his daughter was nearby, languishing petrified in the clutches of some thoroughly nasty kidnappers in the cause of a salutary learning experience.

Sir Hades was up early for breakfast — this was not the influence of his work ethic, this was all about getting as much food inside him as he could while at the Hôtel de Paris.

After breakfast he changed into his ninja pants and

black ninja pyjamas, slung a katana samurai sword on his back and met up with his driver who took the spectacular sea road to the small and excruciatingly beautiful farm where he had arranged for the kidnappers to hold his daughter.

The world's press were camped outside like a besieging medieval army. The zoom lenses and TV camera lenses and microphone booms and satellite dishes positively bristled with anticipation in the morning sun. The event was being shown in real time on Ustream and The Guardian was running a live blog. With such an army behind him, Hades didn't stand a chance of not having his exploits splashed across the news all over the world. Penguins in Antarctica wouldn't be able to miss this event.

Hilda Titanium stepped from the throng to greet Hades. She was clad in a full burqa so the press would keep their attention on the farm, not her.

'Is the glare of publicity sufficiently dazzling?'

'Oh, I'll say. Splendid job. Thank you very much. I like the Hades Underwear logo on the front of the house. Nice touch.'

Hilda adjusted Hades' ninja costume making sure that the Hades logos thereon were similarly conspicuous.

'No trouble at all. Now, you go and kick some serious bottom.'

Hades unsheathed his katana and led the charge of camera crews up the driveway. He kicked in the front door (workmen had previously installed an easily kick-down-able door) and barged into the house.

There was no sign of kidnappers or kidnapped in the kitchen so he charged on into the living room. Nothing there, either. He charged swooshing his weapon up the stairs and through the bedrooms and back downstairs, where he paused nonplussed until he remembered the basement. Of course! The basement! Kidnappers always hang out in basements. He should have started with the basement.

And so with a manly bellow he stormed the basement and had impaled a dart board on his sword before he realised that this place too was devoid of his daughter or the people he had paid a lot of money to put her here.

He went back through the house peeking in the pantry and all the wardrobes and closets and came up with nothing.

Oh, buggery bugger-bags, he thought. Did he have the wrong address?

'Ms Titanium? There would appear to be no kidnap here. Do we have the right address?'

'Yes, we certainly do, Sir Hades. However, there was a note pinned to the front door which you charged right over, the contents of which might provide some illumination.'

She proffered Sir Hades a big brown envelope that was very crumpled and covered in boot marks.

The note inside was made up of letters cut from newspapers and magazines and it said: *We have your daughter. Do not contact the police, the media, or Gnash and Grr. Prepare a million squillion spondulicks in unmarked, used bills. We will issue instructions on what to do with the money. Any failure to comply with these demands and we will eat Victoria.*

'Turn those bloody cameras off! There's been a kidnapping!'

His ninja underpants accidentally went off and a CNN cameraman toppled with a shuriken in his forehead.

12

'Victoria's been kidnapped,' Sir Hades bawled into his phone. He was back at the Hôtel de Paris being rubbed down by flunkies with hot towels.

'I know. You told me that yesterday,' said Persephone, hundreds of miles away in Britain.

'Yes, but she's even more kidnapped today than she was yesterday. I just came down here to the south of France to rescue her and she was gone. Kidnapped.'

'Sort of double kidnapped then? That's very careless of you Hades, losing our one and only daughter twice in one week and the second time right on the cusp of rescue. And was the world's media there to see you lose her? How very humiliating for you.'

'You're taking this very calmly, Persephone.'

'Yes, it's a quality I have finally learned from you. I've learned such a lot from you, darling, especially in the last couple of days. Well, I dare say she'll turn up. Kidnap victims usually do eventually, in one state of decay or other. I'll let you get on with the search, then darling. I suggest you get back to it as soon as possible. France is a very large country. And if you can't find her there, this planet has several huge continents to scour. Please leave no stone unturned.'

She rang off and luxuriated a bit more in her capacious and frothing bathtub.

'Let the bastard stew,' she said to the replica Manneken Pis, the Belgian peeing boy statue, which was streaming Moet into the tub. 'I'm just giving him a taste of his own medicine. Very clever really. Maul and Flay should be arriving here any moment with Victoria safe and sound, while my scheming husband worries himself silly in France. And bloody serves him right for scaring the living daylights out of our Vicky. Just one more smidgeon-sized tot of champers and I'll get on the go.'

13

Sir Hades stared very forlornly at his phone while the flunkies buffed and rubbed away with the hot towels.

'What have I done?'

'Not to worry sir, we didn't smell a thing.'

'What? No, I —'

'Think nothing of it, sir. We are professionals and very discreet with it. Would you like us to check for any flecks that might have escaped with it?'

'What? No, I mean what have I done? I've lost my daughter.'

'That's a cute euphemism, sir. I shall have to remember it.'

'No, I really have lost my daughter.'

'Oh yes, I really will have to remember it.'

'One minute my daughter was with Maul and Flay and the next all of them were gone. But where? How? Why?'

'That's a not just a euphemism, Sir Hades, that is a deep and complex metaphor. It will go down well in Paris.'

'I wonder whether it's time to call Gnash and Grr.'

'Whoa! Definitely sounds like flecks, I think. I will get the rubber tweezers.'

14

By about sundowner time, Persephone Gousset was very much aware of the absence of Victoria, Maul and Flay. If absence could have mass and scale and make scary noises, this absence would have been about the size and shape and sound of Godzilla.

'Where can they be?' she asked the Manneken Pis, forgetting it wasn't sentient.

'They were supposed to be here hours ago. It's not that far from the south of France. Is it? Look, give me a top up and I'll make some calls.'

Persephone started by calling the private jet. This turned out to be still waiting at Nice Côte d'Azur airport.

'This is not good,' she told Manneken.

She called Maul and Flay's phone, but all she got was a message that the number was unavailable. She checked their Facebook page. The status read, *Nowhere to be found. Mwah ha ha ha ha!*

'My god, Victoria's been kidnapped!' She smashed the Mannekin's head off with a karate kick and champagne gushed all over the bathroom.

15

Zip.

'Are you really letting me out of the bag?'

'No, not really. We're just checking if you're still alive.'

'And what if I am still alive?'

'We'll zip you up in the bag again.'

'And if I'm not still alive?'

'We'll zip you up in the bag again.'

'So, this is an academic exercise, a bit like the Schrödinger's cat experiment.'

'No, not a bit. The cat was in a box. You are in a bag. Not the same thing at all.'

Zip.

16

After Maul had stuffed Victoria into the bag those — how many? — nights ago at Villa Parque, the bag had been dumped in the back of a vehicle of some kind which drove very fast on winding cliff roads through the night. The vehicle veered perilously close to the precipice on many of the tight bends, which would have compounded Victoria's fear had she been aware. However, her fear was fully engaged with what she knew of her predicament; with being trapped, with Timmy being dead, with her now being thrown around on a lurching flatbed with rolling tyre irons and bottles and what smelled like a dead cat, but which was a pair of Maul's underpants.

She screamed and cursed her way into near-insensibility.

Had she been privy to the front seats of the four-wheel drive she would have seen and heard Maul and Flay discussing her.

'Can I nail her to the railway sleeper in the back to stop her rolling about?'

'No.'

'I mean nail her, not the bag, to the sleeper.'

'No.'

'Can I cut her ears off and force them into her mouth to shut her up?'

'No.'

'Can I bludgeon her with the tyre iron for no particular reason at all?'

'No.'

'Isn't this a proper kidnapping?'

'No. And bury those underpants when we get back.'

'I find the smell of them put the tracker dogs off.'

'True, but I wonder whether avoiding 20 years in prison is worth the pain of that smell.'

Eventually, the vehicle arrived wherever it was headed. The bag was removed from the car and put somewhere else and she was let out, but the letting out didn't help very much because it was pitch black and Victoria couldn't see a thing. She could well have been in a much bigger bag, one that was big enough to walk around in and which contained large solid objects on which she could bark her shins.

Heavy footsteps and the banging of doors and the clattering of bolts told her that the two abductors had left and that she was well and truly incarcerated.

17

With dawn she found that she was in some kind of basement. The morning light peeked in curiously from small windows above her head but gave nothing away. The walls were rustically hewn from ancient wood and rock. So, she was evidently still in the south of France where everything is rustic and adorable, even the dens of kidnappers.

The large implacable objects in which she had barked her shins in the night turned out to be the obligatory denizens of basements: a washing machine and a dryer and some kind of stove, the kind that's handy for burning body parts.

There were also several large trunks and piles and piles of assorted junk as if the basement were suffering an existential crisis and thought itself an attic. Mounted on one of the supporting columns was a dartboard, which would come in handy later.

Victoria creaked cautiously up the noisy stairway to the door. The door, in the time-honoured tradition of prisons, was locked. Very locked, and made of a sturdy wood that sort of stood implacably and stared at her in a way that said: "Don't even think about trying to open me. I don't move, me, not even for the heiresses of the fabulously wealthy."

On tiptoe, she crept just as noisily down the stairs and

dragged and bothered the basement junk into piles that she could climb to get to the windows, which, in another time-honoured tradition had bars on them. And more big locks — locks that were just as implacable as the basement door and which said "Fuck off!" in a big, implacable voice.

Victoria then explored all the corners and the spaces behind the junk and as much as possible under the junk in the hope there may be a secret trap door or the entrance to an enchanted world or a hole leading to a badger set, or perhaps a key for the door or just a big battering ram.

She found no such things; her kidnappers had well and truly kidnapped her.

Victoria sat on a trunk in order to despair better.

There was a tremendous rattling and thumping and clanging from the top of the stairs and the door opened. Her two captors appeared and started down the stairs, which had merely creaked horribly when Victoria had used and now screamed horrendously as if in pain.

The two figures looked pretty much as they had the night before. One tall and thin and exuding iciness. The other short and round and exuding drool and smells and ickiness.

'We've brought you something to eat,' said the tall one with a tone you would normally expect to accompany a declaration that the victim was about to be sawn in half, lengthwise, without anaesthetic and starting at the most sensitive part of the anatomy.

Maul carrying a tray the size of a car park cleared some space on a trunk with his foot and set the food down. Ham, salami, a dozen cheeses, salad, crusty bread, terrine, and olives.

'I'm sorry it's only good stuff,' said Maul. 'This is France and they only have good stuff. I couldn't get any baked beans or kebab.'

It may have been good food to Maul, but to Victoria it was merely normal. She didn't know what baked beans or kebabs were and wasn't at all sure what point Maul had been making. 'No wine?' she asked.

'I'm not whining, I'm just saying,' said Maul.

'You may be feeling a little cold and vulnerable dressed — or undressed — as you are,' said Flay in a tone that now suggested she was going to rub salt on the blade before sawing Victoria in half. 'I got you these.'

Flay tossed Victoria some grey things that might have been sackcloth. Unravelled, they turned out to be a set of hideous sweats.

'What are these?' asked a mystified Victoria.

'Clothes.'

'They don't look like clothes to me. Clothes are things you put on your body and they have brands and stuff. These look like the things the hounds sleep on.'

'They are the sort of clothes that poor people wear. People who have no money.'

Victoria stopped and wrinkled up her pretty little nose, which in her was a sign of thinking. 'People with no money? Like the Queen? I hear she never carries money and yes, she does wear a lot of brown and stuff doesn't she.'

'I got them from the naff stuff bin at the charity store. One euro. If you cover up, my assistant here might stop masturbating for a moment and keep his mind on his job.'

Maul removed his hands from his pockets with a protesting moan as Victoria quickly wiggled into the clothes.

'My, don't you look the little princess,' said Flay. 'The little kidnapped princess.'

'Princess? I thought I might look like the Queen in this. Is there a mirror in here? Do I look like the Queen?'

'Oh, yes, you look exactly like the Queen.' Flay placed the fingers of one hand on Maul's head and twisted so that he turned to face the way out. She gave him a little shove and up the stairs he clumped.

'Now, look here,' said Victoria in her best taking command voice. 'About letting me go. Do it now. I won't stand for this. I really won't.'

Flay's laugh sounded like an iceberg sheering from a glacier and sliding into the ocean.

'Neither will my father stand for it. Do you have any

idea who my father is?'

Again, Flay laughed in her catastrophic way. The sound like a broken drain gurgling behind her was probably Maul joining in.

'Well, I'll tell you, my father is a multi-mega-squillionaire and he'll pay whatever it takes to get me out of here.'

The horrible cacophony in the basement suggested that both Flay and Maul were further amused by this revelation.

'And then he'll hire some of those weird hench-people he keeps for unsavoury jobs and who we're not supposed to know about and they'll track you down and do all sorts of horrible and unsavoury things to you so you completely regret that you ever even heard of me.'

Maul's gurgling drain became a gushing sinkhole and Flay's entire glacier slipped into the ocean.

'Just you see.'

Maul and Flay, still making their awful noises left their captive to herself.

And so began Victoria's incarceration.

18

To be fair, neither Maul nor Flay either mauled or flayed her. They brought plentiful amounts of food and drink. Flay would appear and disappear with an economy of word and movement. Maul liked to hang about scratching his parts and staring at Victoria while she ate. He didn't partake of the picnics himself. Maul would eat bits of himself or bits of stuff he had extracted from his own orifices. He didn't say much that was intelligible but he would rummage in his clothes in an alarming way and whimper from time to time.

Neither did Maul or Flay speak much to each other. They seemed to have an odd relationship. The longest exchange she heard between them was:

'Go on, let me.'

To which Flay replied, 'Get back to your basket, you filthy animal,'

'Aw! Why?'

'Because if you foul up this cushy little earner, I'll feed you to the pigs and I'll skip the bit where I euthanise you first.'

'Thank you.'

Conditions could have been worse. The kidnappers arranged a nice little camp bed. The basement had its own loo, which Victoria thought was very civilised until she realised Maul was sneaking in to lick it clean every time she used it.

Victoria's main enemy during this captivity was boredom.

There was no one to talk to unless you counted Maul and Flay. She had counted them. More than once. There were two of them, and no matter how many times she counted them that there were never more or less than two or them.

She had no mobile phone, so she couldn't call anyone. There was, incredibly, no computer or tablet so that meant no Facebook or YouTube or shopping. There was no TV — how was that even possible? There were no restaurants, nightclubs or parties. There were no expensive shops selling branded clothes or bags or jewellery, so that doubly meant no shopping. In fact, there were no shops of any kind. No skiing holidays or exotic beaches or yachts and not one single Venice. There were no servants or small yappy dogs. Really, how did people in cellars even survive?

To mark time Victoria drew lines on the wall: four parallel lines tied together in a bunch of five with a diagonal line. The four walls were covered in these marks. Not because she had been kept captive for several years but because she scratched a line on the wall whenever she thought to herself that she was bored which was pretty much right after drawing each line. She was unaware that prisoners usually used this drawing-line device to count whole days, the passing of which could gauged from the alternating of day and night.

There was an old deflated football in the cellar too, but no football players, old, deflated, or otherwise. She imagined it was a huge meatball on a plate of spaghetti and that she would eat it if she became bored of crusty baguettes and Mimolet and salami.

She was strengthened by the thought that her father would soon have her out of there.

Where on earth was he?

She had no idea why Maul and Flay had grabbed her but was confident that her father would pay whatever it took to get her out. Or come and get her himself.

There was a dartboard in the cellar but, frustratingly, no darts. Victoria eventually hit on the idea of imagining throwing darts at the board. At first she was terrible and kept missing. She could never hit the red spot in the middle but after lots and lots of practice she could occasionally imagine hitting the number one. Once she had got to that level of competence, she began to imagine hitting the number two after the number one. After hours and hours of laborious practice, she began to try for three, four, five and six. She couldn't go further than that because she couldn't count further.

Then, she hit a run and thudded her imaginary darts into the board in quick succession, 1, 2, 3, 4, 5, 6 and then 7. She stopped, puzzled. How did she know that 7 was the next number? She was sure 7 was the number after 6. It felt right. She then threw 8 and 9. That felt right too. But what just happened? Why was she able to count only to 6 one minute and then to 9 the next?

Before she could think further about this mystery or figure out what number came after 9, her captors clomped back into the cellar.

'Time for a little trip, princess,' and she was back in the bag again.

19

The next journey was very long indeed. It just went on and on and on, and then when it had finished going on and on and on, it went on and on and on some more.

This journey wasn't like the first she had taken with Maul and Flay the night she was abducted. On that occasion the bag was hurled around as the car careened along narrow and winding mountain roads. And there had been that appalling and disturbing smell. That otherworldly, evil pong that was bad enough to get dogs howling and gagging, a smell bad enough to get the denizens of Hell running for the exits if it had been unleashed in the inferno.

No, this journey was quite different. The roads were faster and straighter. This was no mountain, precipice-defying dash. Victoria guessed this was a big, modern motorway that whisked you from one big conurbation to another.

Maul and Flay — most likely Maul, protesting, under the instructions of Flay — had placed an airbed or something under Victoria's bag. All together, she was far less likely to be beaten to death by this journey.

However, it was long. Terribly, terribly long and a bit longer than that. In terms of boredom, this was worse than the cellar. There was no dartboard for imaginary darts. No football for imaginary spaghetti dishes and the chances of a good shopping spree or peeled grape were even more remote

Victoria's captors were having a less awful time. Not confined in bags but sitting comfortably up front, they had the luxury of photons and distraction. Had Victoria been privy to the front seats, she would have heard Maul and Flay having the following conversation.

'I spy with my little eye, something beginning with m.'
'Motorway.'
'Nope.'
'Map.'
'Nope.'
'Matchstick.'
'Nope.'
'Magazine.'
'Nope.'
'Mamba.'
'Nope.'
'I give up. What is it?'
'Embankment.'
'Embankment is not an m.'
'Yes it is. *Em*bankment. Right. I spy with my little eye, something beginning with another m.'
'Moron.'
'Nope.'
'Moulins.'
'Nope.'
'Mountain.'
'Nope.'
'Moon.'
'Nope.'
'Muzzle.'
'Nope.'
'Maintenent.'
'Nope.'
'Magnate's daughter trussed in the back of this pickup.'
'Nope. But close.'
'Money.'
'Nope. But not a million miles off.'

'A million squillion spondulicks.'
'Nope. But scaldingly close.'
'For Christ's sake, I give up. What?'
'Maul's a clever bastard.'
'Is that it? Is that your m?'
'It's my best m, that one.' Maul looked very smug and proud.

20

The ambient sounds changed and so did the movement of the car. From going straight and fast, they seemed to be going in slow circles. Victoria guessed they were in Paris.

Had Victoria been privy to the conversation in the front of the car, she would have heard.

'Are you serious?'
'Oh, yes.'
'No way!'
'Oh, most definitely.'
'Brilliant!'
'Well, it's the kind of place people keep valuables, isn't it. And I don't think they'll let her in a numbered Swiss bank account, will they.'
'Ace. It's just like a real kidnapping.'
'It most certainly is.'

Finally the car parked and she felt herself being carried. Wherever they were, the acoustics, such as she could hear them were expansive and echoing. At least they were until she felt herself being shoved into a confined space and all sound was abruptly cut off at the same time something heavy bumped her on the head.

She has been stashed in a coin locker if she is not mistaken. She is not mistaken.

Victoria had plenty of time to think while in the bag. She had plenty of time to think she might suffocate. She had oodles of time to think she might be tossed in a river or in the sea. She had a seeming aeon to think about starving to death, dying of thirst, being dropped from a great height, placed in the path of a train, being sold to slavers, being passed to organ dealers or vivisectionists, being shot into space, being made into dim sum or of simply being forgotten somewhere at the back of a closet and found years later during spring cleaning by someone who would make a tut-tutting sound and who would say, "Now, who left that there?"

The inside of a bag without a clue what is going on around you is not a place for repose. And whoever put her there, she decided, was going to get a severe thumping when she got out.

21

'Hello.'

'This is Hades Gousset. Is this Gnash or Grr?'

'Is this is a test?'

'No.'

'Because if the subject is Hades Gousset, as in 'This is Hades Gousset,' then neither of the choices of subject in the follow up question, "Is this Gnash or Grr?" are equivalent to Hades Gousset, so the answer must be neither. The answer must be Hades Gousset. Except that choice was not offered. Was it a trick question?'

'No, I mean, am I speaking to Gnash or Grr?'

'I know what you meant. I was making a point about logic, that's what I was doing. Call yourself an underpants magnate? With thinking skills like that you're not qualified to be a fridge magnet.'

'I see. Very clever. Which the fuck are you? Not that I care. It was a pro forma question.'

'That's more like it. Dropping the slimy and insincere façade of business bonhomie for the true face of laissez faire viciousness. Excellent. Getting to the truth of things now.'

'Some piece of worm poop has kidnapped my daughter and I'm offering enough dosh to fill a flotilla of dreamboats to anyone who can help me get her back — preferably with extreme violence inflicted on the kidnappers, and the anyone I specifically have in mind is Messrs Gnash and Grr. Are you in?'

'Taking us for granted now, are we? Trading in glib stereotypes, are we? Treating us like two-dimensional cut outs of ourselves now, is it?'

'What?'

'So, what you really think is that Gnash and Grr respond solely to money and opportunities to inflict pain.'

'You could only have been more succinct if you had just shut up and listened to the proposal.'

'Well, you've got us wrong. Let me tell you that.'

'What?'

'No. We're not merely mercenary. There's more to us than that.'

'Fine.'

'In fact, we are out of the business for good.'

'I see. I did say there was boatloads of money in this. I can't really do better than that because I can't think of anything bigger than lots of boats for carrying money around.'

'We are, in fact, recently out of the business.'

'Which business? Murder, extortion or mayhem?'

'Very extremely funny. We have, in fact, just given up all the above and gone into a new line of work, a profession that better reflects the depths of our souls and psyches. One that expresses our true selves.'

'Gratuitous impaling of live victims on sharpened rampikes? A bloke called Vlad has already done it.'

'No, we've opened a shop.'

'A shop?'

'Yes. A shop. And we've opened it on Rue Du Bain. That's in Preston. An aromatherapy shop. It's stocked chock-a-block with aromas and therapies, both. You'll love it. So, I'm sorry we can't help you. Fuck off.' Grr rang off.

Gnash, reclining on a chintz sofa, sucking aroma sticks asked, 'Who was that?'

'Gousset.'

'What did he want?'

'Some piece of worm poo has kidnapped his daughter,

apparently.'
'Why didn't we think of that?'
'I think we just did.'

22

'Damn, fuck, buggery bugger-bags and arse-wank!' exploded Sir Hades Gousset momentarily before slamming his telephone in the bathroom sink and beating it to death with his forehead.

23

'They've been in contact, Sir Hades. Hmm, do you think I could have some pureed telephone while you are there. Looks delish,' said Hilda Titanium arriving unannounced.

The Hotel de Paris flunkies rubbing down Sir Hades boggled their eyes at Hilda and immediately applied the hot towels to themselves.

'I am totally naked, Hilda.'

'I wouldn't have noticed if you hadn't pointed it out. Shall I go away and come back when you've had another family member abducted?'

'Garçon, or whatever your name is, leave yourself alone and give me a towel to cover myself … Oh, never mind, I'll use your toupee. Right. What have you got.'

'I infer from the state of your telephone that you had a good chat with Gnash and Grr. That'll help.'

'They've opened an aromatherapy centre. In Preston.'

'Even better. The kidnappers have told us they'll make the switch in Disneyland Paris. Tomorrow afternoon. Four o'clock.'

'In Disneyland? What on earth for? Are they mad?'

'Well, yes, they are mad. We know that because they crossed you.'

'Scoundrels!'

'Scoundrels? That's a little mild coming from you.'

'They're scoundrels for being mad. They're

unspeakable blaggards for snatching my daughter and wanting to make the exchange in Disneyland.'

'That's more like it. Well, I think they thought Disneyland would make a nice day out. Make the switch and then catch a ride on It's a Small World. One needs to kick back after committing a heinous crime.'

Hades began to see the way the kidnappers were thinking. 'There are also lots of people around. Witnesses to any confrontations. Crowds to blend in with. Lots of movement and colour and sudden noises to confuse the senses. Families, kids, balloons; potential embarrassing collateral damage if we take direct action. Hideous bad taste to keep you off balance.'

'Not that we are thinking for even an iota of a nano-instant of doing anything other than playing the game and getting our daughter back in one piece.' It was Persephone who had just swept into the room with a retinue of assistants, lawyers, accountants, ex-special forces contractors with bags of money and Catshit the PA, covered in dirt and wriggling worms, all of whom now paused to take in the tableaux of several Hotel de Paris flunkies assaulting themselves with hot towels, Hilda Titanium in stunning sackcloth and Hades Gousset shading his private parts with a toupee, all framed by the Cathedral-like opulence of the most expensive bathroom of the most expensive hotel in Monaco.

'We can't let these baboons get away with this. How dare they threaten our daughter's life?' boomed Hades.

'How dare you risk our daughter's life with a simple-minded scheme for revenge to assuage your impugned pride?' replied Persephone.

'Oh. So you're adamant about that are you, darling?'

'Immaculately so, dearest.'

'So that's settled then. We'll capitulate meekly and give them a bonus for being so ever-so bad.'

'Reason reigns. You will stay within my sight at all times from now on and until our Victoria is safely retrieved. Then, and only then, may you go forth and rain molten retribution on the heads of these pieces of worm poo.'

'The matter seems to be settled then. Very good. As the tiniest matter of curiosity, how did you know about the exchange tomorrow?' Hades asked his good lady.

'They contacted me at the same time as they contacted you. Probably as a means of making sure there was a functioning brake on your desire to charge straight into violence.'

'As I say, blaggards.'

'May I make a suggestion?' It was Catshit who was having a problem containing a desire to stick his oar in.

'Do you have to?'

'Well, it might prevent me wetting the floor.'

'Go on then,' sighed Hades.

'Well. I have a plan that might completely obviate the risks inherent in going through with this exchange with its vagaries and unknowns.'

'Are you going to say something that will cause me to want to eat this toupee in frustration?'

'I imagine so, sir.'

'And I doubt there's much I can do about it. So. What's the plan?'

'These kidnappers. They are obviously motivated by money, aren't they. I mean, they were paid first to simply fake a kidnapping but when they were offered more money to fake a second kidnapping they accepted the more money without apparent qualm. And it was probably at this point in time they realised that, having taken two lots of money, one larger than the other, they could now have a real kidnapping, asking an amount of money hugely more than the two they had already received.'

So far so embarrassing. 'So what's your point, Catshit?'

'Why don't we buy them off? Pay them money to give Ms Victoria back? In short, pay them to stop kidnapping her.'

'So we pay the kidnappers to release Victoria?'

'Indeed. Driven by venality, they won't be able to say no.'

'Rather than paying the kidnappers to release Victoria,

which is the current plan.'

'Absolutely, sir.'

'Catshit. Get back to fertilising the rhubarb, please,' said Hilda.

'Very good, ma'am.'

Catshit left and silence reigned.

'Persephone, dear. I can't help noticing that you are staring at me with a quality usually denoted by the adverb "intently", while nothing in particular is happening.'

'Yes, Hades. I'm keeping you in my sight so that you don't do anything silly.'

'And are you going to stare at me like this, in this bathroom until four o'clock tomorrow afternoon?'

'Knowing you, dear, I think that it will be precisely necessary.'

24

After a very long time in the station coin locker, Victoria experienced being moved again, and again inferred location and mode of transport through motion and muffled sound. To her it felt like: a car through city streets, then a pony and trap through New England countryside; now a bucking dragon in the skies of China, transferring to a tunnel trolley in the mines of Mordor; and onto a spaceship tearing from the grip of earth's gravity to slingshot around Alpha Centauri before depositing her on a slow camel on the dunes of the Sahara, and from there a train from Charles de Gaulle Etoile station to Disneyland, just outside Paris.

Victoria guessed they were at Disneyland because she thought she heard Maul arguing with Mickey Mouse.

'Let us in, Mickey.'

'Bonjour, monsieur. Comment puis-je vous aider?'

'Let us in! Open the frog-eating gate!'

'Quel genre de billet voulez-vous? Et pour combien de personnes? Avez-vous déjà des billets avec l'un de nos forfaits spéciaux? Avez-vous réservé en ligne? Avez-vous des e-tickets? Ou aimeriez-vous acheter des billets maintenant? Si oui, êtes-vous une famille? Il y a un prix spécial pour les familles. Si vous êtes un groupe, vous pouvez obtenir des billets pour quatre jours pour tous les domaines pour le prix de trois jours? Cela représente toute une économie, monsieur.' Of course, this wasn't Mickey. It sounded to Victoria like a nice young man with spectacles sitting in his Disney ticket booth, asking about Maul's Disney-related needs and setting out his many happy options. And Victoria was completely right, right down to the spectacles. The nice young man with spectacles had been saying, "What kind of ticket would you like, and for how many people? Do you have tickets already with one of our special packages? Did you book online? Do you have e-tickets? Or would you like to buy tickets now? If so, are you a family? There is a special family price. If you are a group, you can get four days of tickets to all areas for the price of three days? That's quite a saving, sir."

'No, you're not listening. We're British and we're coming through. You remember that Napoleon Bonehead? Well, look what happened to him when he got in the way of the British when we were coming through.'

The nice young Disney man had met English louts before and was not to be diverted from his mission to offer the best possible service. 'Eh bien, comme je vous le demandais, pour combien de personnes et quel genre de plan voulez-vous obtenir, monsieur? Il y a effectivement un hôtel à l'intérieur du parc et nous proposons des offres fantastiques qui combinent l'entrée et l'hébergement.' Or, "Well, as I was saying, how many people, and what kind of plan, would you like, sir? There is actually a hotel inside the park and we do some fantastic deals on combinations of passes and accommodation."

Maul, on the other hand had met polite and reasonable people before and was not put off his mission to be as gratuitously unreasonable and obnoxious as possible. 'Look. We're on important British business and it's our right to go wherever, or you are guilty of holding up the necessary movement of capital in a free market economy and therefore of causing an economic slowdown. So get with the plan, garlic hair, and open the frigging gate. Ze friggin' gate, ¿Entiendes?'

There are more things in heaven and earth than are dreamed of by Maul's measly little brain — an infinity of things he has no conception of — and one of them was talking to him now. 'Je comprends chaque mot que vous dites, mon pote. Je parle probablement l'anglais mieux que vous. Je viens de Bristol et je suis étudiant à l'University College de Londres. Je fais un job d'été tout en améliorant mon français. Je n'ai pas l'intention de vous parler autre qu'en français jusqu'à ce que vous montriez un peu de putain de respect.'

Or, as Maul was unable and unwilling to comprehend, "I understand every word you are saying, pal. I probably speak English better than you do. I'm from Bristol and a student of University College London. I'm doing a summer job and polishing my French at the same time. I have no intention of speaking anything other than French to you until you show some fucking respect."

'Oh, yeah? Oh, yeah? You reckon? You're not telling me Goofy paid to get in here, so schnell, schnell, open that fucking gate.'

The young man with the spectacles smiled sweetly. 'Je suis payé pour m'asseoir et vous parler et je peux le faire aussi longtemps que mon service dure ou jusqu'à ce que j'appuie sur le bouton rouge qui aura pour effet de rassembler tout une bande d'agents de sécurité très brutaux. Alors qu'est-ce que vous choisissez? Payer ou être battu?' — "I'm being paid to sit talking to you and can do so as long as my shift lasts or until I press the red button that will summon a gang of very brutal security guards. So what's it to be? Pay up or get beaten up?"

'I have already told you, Mickey, mate. Open ze friggin gate or I'll shove Sleeping Beauty's Castle right up your bum sideways.'

'Et comment vous allez faire ça si je ne vous laisse pas passer?' — "And how will you do that when I won't let you in?"

Flay enjoyed the spectacle of Maul digging this hole he would never get out of but the prospect of collecting a million-squillion ill-gotten spondulicks was even more compelling. She decided to intervene and move things along. 'Je m'excuse de la part de mon collègue. Il a une gueule bien trempée et le cerveau d'un abruti.' — "I apologise for my colleague. He has the mouth of a toilet and the brain of a turd."

'Heureux de l'entendre. Donc, ce n'était pas mon imagination.' — "Glad to hear it. So it wasn't my hallucination."

'Non, je crains que non. C'est comme ça partout où il va. C'est un voyou professionnel, vous savez.' — "No, I'm afraid not. He's like this wherever he goes. He's a professional hoodlum, you know."

'Quelle surprise!'

'Eh bien, pouvons-nous avoir des billets pour trois adultes, s'il vous plaît? — "Well, can we have tickets for three adults, please?"

'Trois? Etes-vous sûr?' — "Three? Are you sure?"

'Oh, oui. La troisième personne est dans le sac ici.' — "Oh, yes. The third one is in the bag here."

'Dans le sac ?' — "In the bag?"

'Oui, elle souffre d'agoraphobie mais elle aime l'idée que nous l'emmenons à Disneyland.' — "Yes, she has agoraphobia but she likes the idea we are taking her to Disneyland."

'C'est très gentil de votre part. Voici vos billets. Je vous souhaite une merveilleuse journée.' — "That's very nice of you. Here are your tickets. I hope you have a nice day."

'That showed him. Slimy frog. What did you tell him?'

'I told him you had the mouth of a toilet and the brain of a turd.'

'Nice one. That showed him. Ha!'

'Right. It's just after 3:00.'

'Time for a quick go on It's a Small World. Can we? Can we? Can we, huh?'

25

Disneyland was glad to see all its visitors. It sang and chirruped and danced around. It whooshed and whirled and did the whirligig. It blew kisses and bubbles and the minds of the happy families that crowded there.

Persephone proceeded through the crowds with the million squillion spondulicks in a large overnight bag which she dragged on a flatbed trolley. A million squillion needs a mighty big bag, one about the size of an oil tanker, and no such bag was to be found on the face of this earth.

Hades had pointed this out to the kidnappers, who had conveniently provided a suitably evil email address: maulandflay@wormpoo.com. The kidnappers responded to put as much cash as possible in the biggest bag they could find and send the balance by PayPal.

Persephone spoke into the cuff of her sleeve: 'I'm approaching the exchange point. So far so good.'

'What's she doing?' asked Hades of Hilda Titanium in their secret control room, which was, in fact, a plastic elephant on the Dumbo ride. Persephone had liked the idea of installing her husband on the Dumbo ride, where, if he didn't get airsick or elephant-sick, he could watch the proceedings without being able to interfere. She had paid the operators to keep the ride in the air for a full hour so her husband couldn't get out.

'She's speaking into her sleeve.'

'Why's she doing that?'

'I imagine it's because that's what people in films do in situations like this.'

'Isn't there supposed to be a microphone in the sleeve when you speak into it?'

'Yes, indeed. I don't suppose she realises that. She says, by the way, that she's approaching the point of exchange.'

'How do you know she said that if there's no microphone in her sleeve?'

'I bugged her hat. I hid a small camera in there too, which is live streaming to the mirror in my compact. Look. And I am listening by means of a fake babelfish inserted in my ear.'

'You cunning devil. Can we communicate with her?'

'Oh yes, I have a microphone cunningly hidden inside a banana, which streams to a speaker hidden in the mouth of her fox fur. All I need to do is hold the banana to my mouth. People will think I'm eating the banana or talking to the banana or having sex with it. No one will guess I'm speaking out of the mouth of a dead fox draped on a middle-aged lady pulling a million squillion spondulicks on a trolley in the middle of Disneyland, which we wouldn't want people to think.'

'Oh. You mean the banana in your bag? The one with "Do not eat" inscribed on it in black eyeliner.'

'That's the one. How did you know I had a banana in my bag?'

'Sorry about that. I was feeling a bit hungry and went looking in your bag for a hand towel to swallow, you know, to fill the hole. Saw the banana, and thought, hello, that'll do nicely. I ate a hand towel as well, just to be safe.'

'Eat your own bloody hand towels!'

'I did. Finished them this morning. That was the problem.'

Persephone, meanwhile, had arrived at the swap spot, which was a fake bench thing. It was a safe bet that the bench was fake because it was in Disneyland. Disneyland is a fastidiously crafted, immersive fantasy world, which meant the bench was, if anything, a bench immersed in a fantasy of its own existence.

She laughed hideously and insanely and twitched until the family sitting there ran away and she made herself comfortable, parking her trolley alongside and arranging her furs about her with fastidious care, looking in the process like a mad old mother bear preparing to do things to people for porridge-related-offences, which, in a sense, she was.

Appearing like a pall of death at a kiddies' picnic, Maul and Flay emerged from the crowd. Maul had a large holdall on his shoulder, which was struggling. A small child passing too close skidded and upended in a pool of his drool. Her father turned on Maul as if about to remonstrate but seeing in Maul's slobber a presentiment of his own messy demise, thought better of confrontation and whisked his daughter away to the medical facilities to be de-salivated.

'Here they come,' said Hades.

'Here they come,' said Persephone's fox stole. The microphone secreted in the banana was now lodged in Hades' epiglottis, which had the potential for great embarrassment for the rest of his life.

Maul and Flay had already thoroughly surveyed the area looking for signs of ambush or double cross and had found none.

'I spy with my little eye,' said Maul, 'something beginning with t.'

'Two clever bastards,' said Flay, 'for bringing Madam Gousset in on the deal as a restraining influence on Monsieur Gousset's capacity for extreme and impulsive violence.'

'Uncanny. Got it in one.'

'Let us continue with twisting the world around our little finger.'

'I haven't got a little finger. I only have a sausage.'

'That'll do.'

They took seats either side of Persephone, and the bench's little fantasy existence suddenly became hideously real.

'The rain in Spain stays mainly on the plane,' said Persephone carefully while pretending to ignore both Maul and Flay.

'The trains in Bahrain go mainly down the drain,' responded Maul equally carefully.

Persephone couldn't help asking, 'What kind of security phrase thing is that?'

'A fucking brilliant one,' said Maul. 'I thought of it myself. While having a dump.'

'Incredible, I'm sure,' said Persephone. 'Do you have my daughter?'

Flay replied, taking charge before her colleague sent the whole deal the way of Bahrain's trains. 'Of course. She's in the bag.'

'How do I know she's alive?'

'The deal didn't specify dead or alive,' said Flay.

'How do I know that's my daughter in the bag and not a decoy?'

'Don't you know your own daughter when you see her? What kind of mother are you?'

'She didn't look like a bag before you got her.'

'The name of the person in the bag,' said Flay, enunciating very carefully, 'is Victoria Gousset.'

'Yes, that's my daughter! No doubt about it! I'd know that name anywhere!'

'OK,' said Flay. 'This is how it works. Maul will put his bag on the trolley next to the loot. He will then casually pick up the identical bag containing the money and saunter, just as casually, away. You will wait until we are out of sight and then take your trolley, exit the park and go away.'

'Identical bags?' The one with the money is blue and the one with my daughter is pink. You didn't say before that the bags should be identical.'

'No one will notice. This is Disneyland.'

'Fine. Let's go for it.'

'Now!' barked the fox round Persephone's neck. 'Go! Go! Go! Go! Go! Go! Last one to put the boot in is a sissy!'

'That's funny,' said Persephone, 'my fox sounds a lot like Hades today. It usually sounds like Hilda Titanium talking into a banana.'

The air was abruptly full of screaming. The kids were screaming, the mums were screaming, the dads were screaming; the grandparents, nephews, nieces, cousins, uncles and aunts were screaming; the delicious roast chickens in the restaurant on the main drag were screaming. I mean, you have to hand it to the French. What they don't know about cleaning up dog poo on the streets of Paris they more than make up for in sheer fucking civilisation. Where in the world can you walk into a tacky, vacuous money-sucker like Disneyland and sit down to dine on an entire half a roast chicken for a couple of euros? The 16 elephants from the Dumbo ride were screaming with the sound of the jet engines installed in their bottoms as they swooped in low over the crowd, firing salvos of peanuts from their trunks. In the lead Dumbo was Hades Gousset and Hilda Titanium, in the others, 30 specially trained psychotics from private violence contractor YellowWater, all armed to the teeth with shotguns, machine guns, big guns, all clad in bullet-proof vests, stab vests, nice woolly vests, wearing night vision goggles, day vision goggles, diving goggles, goggle-eyed goggles, and generally all kitted up and ready for a privately funded but very professional rumpus.

A micro-nano-mite of an inkling after this development registered with everyone in Fantasyland, a barrage of flares and smoke bombs went off turning the air into an exploding marble pudding of orange, red, green, yellow and purple and adding mayhem to the chaos.

The Dumbos flew directly into the thick smoke, unswerving in their mission of rescue and retribution, while Mickey Mouse himself appeared from nowhere and dived into the fray in damsel-saving idiom.

26

The smoke cleared to reveal the predictable pile of crashed Dumbos with its cargo of YellowWater contractors bloodied and dismembered and dangling from the cockpits of their shattered rides.

Hades stood akimbo on top of the struggling but helpless Maul and Flay. Persephone hugged her ecstatic daughter, released from the clutches of these unwholesome evildoers.

'Oh, Mummy, I'm so sorry I faked my own kidnapping for attention and money thereby exposing myself to the risk of a real kidnapping. And Daddy, thank you for rescuing me so heroically. And I'm sorry about the deaths of 30 YellowWater operatives in the process of saving this one undeserving person.'

And Persephone turned to her hubby and exclaimed, 'I forgive you for ignoring my instructions to stay away. You clever man, you have saved our daughter, and brought justice and retribution to the evil curs who took her, and you have saved us a boatload of money in the process. I hope you remembered to cancel the PayPal transfer.'

Spoiling the heroic tableaux a mite was its failure to be real. In actuality, redemption and reconciliation was entirely absent. As was Victoria.

27

Victoria was gone.
Nowhere to be seen.
Vanished.
Disappeared.
'Where's my daughter?' asked Persephone, quite reasonably.
'What?' said Hades, eloquently.
'Victoria. Our daughter. Where is she?' asked Persephone imploringly.
'What?' said Hades, reiteratively.
'Oh, crap,' exclaimed Hilda pithily.

28

'Our daughter's been kidnapped!' wailed Hades and Persephone together.

29

Persephone took the development very well under the circumstances. She kicked over Sleeping Beauty's Castle and jettisoned Space Mountain out of the park and all the way to the moon. She probably would have inserted all the cute dolls of It's a Small World into her husband at great speed had he not anticipated the danger and fled with the insensible Maul and Flay in the last remaining airworthy Dumbo.

30

Sir Hades Gousset retreated to Britain and back to his underwear testing bunker at Pants Down, the facility formerly known as Porton Down.

Porton Down, since it was established during the first world war, has been the British Military's box of secrets. If there is anything that the army, navy or air force don't want people to know about, it's stashed at Porton Down. All the stuff and gadgetry of war since 1916 had been thought of and tested here: all the hardware that goes bang or boom or kaboom. It's not just the noisy stuff that has been tested here. At Porton Down they have developed all the secret stuff, the sorts of things that do a similar job to the bangs, booms and kabooms without making a sound. The military grade SBDs, so to speak.

It is such a secret place that it is here that any stray aliens recovered from UFO test sites are taken. Wikipedia's entry on the place simply states: "Porton Down is so secret it doesn't even exist. So go away and forget you even mistakenly thought it might have existed. We have traced your IP address and we know who you are and where you are and that means we know who your loved ones are and where they are. We have given your name to GCHQ and the NSA. We have put you on the no fly list and taken you off the Christmas list. You have been designated an international terrorist and subversive. Need we say more? Now bugger off."

More recently, when the British government ran out of money and was selling off the army, navy, air force, crown jewels, royal corgis and everything else, it was an obvious purchase for Hades. The secret purposes of this laboratory-cum-testing ground for just about everything was the perfect match for his own business empire, which also dealt with undercover things.

One of Porton Down's more controversial activities over the decades has been testing some of their secrets on animals and people. Once upon a time, one of the things they tested on people was a fangled substance called LSD. History was not clear why the British military thought it needed to test LSD on people in secret when thousands of people every weekend were blatantly testing it on themselves in universities, in parks, at gigs, at parties and probably in the supermarket. Presumably, this is just this sort of thing that makes the military mind remarkable.

By the time Hades acquired the Down, the LSD tests on humans were well in the dark past, discontinued when the boffins discovered that LSD was for fun, not for torment. However, Hades had found, the legacy remained in the form of the test facilities and test staff and subjects — who weren't dummies before their brains crashed in the experiments, but who were very much dummies now.

He found them tonight in the disused test centre, gibbering and drooling and raving and painting rainbows on the walls with their tongues.

'Good evening, gentlemen. I trust you are well. And if not well, then sufficiently bonkers to not care. How would you like to have a bit of fun? Get something back for those peculiar and unnecessary tests on you?'

A scarecrow, one of the former subjects, answered, 'Uhrrrurrrrhuuur ping!'

'Is it a time machine or just a hamster again?' a man in a very threadbare lab coat wanted to know.

'Groovy ectoplasm, man!' declared a smart old soldier in psychedelic battle fatigues.

'Excellent. Follow me. I'd like to introduce you to

Maul and Flay. No, that's a blank wall, sir. Maul and Flay are the things strapped to the table. Perhaps you'd like to work on them. Work on them to what end is up to you. If you should by any chance fish any information out of either of them, throw it back and fish it out again. But please take your time. There's no hurry.'

Rubbing his hands, Hades hurried back to his bunker to begin the process of figuring out what had happened to his daughter.

Hilda Titanium was already there, downloading to the computer the video footage she had taken from the camera in Persephone's hat. It was ready for analysis to establish what had happened to Victoria and the bag of money.

Frame by frame, they studied the Disney crowd and the background for any clue. As Maul and Flay approached there was nothing to be seen. When the first Dumbos detached from the arms of the ride, the picture became very jerky as Persephone tried to take everything in and started to panic.

All Hades and Hilda could see was tourists running for their lives under a rain of peanuts while Maul picked his nose. Next, the smoke bombs went off. They had not been set off by Hades and his crew and now the video suggested they had not come from either Maul or Flay. They just seemed to appear out of nowhere in a sudden barrage. What was that about?

Now Persephone was in a frenzy and her hat had become detached and was spinning through the air. Hades and Hilda rocked on their feet trying to follow the images without being seasick. They glimpsed Hades leaping into shot and pinioning Maul and Flay to the ground. Maul continued to pick his nose.

And that was that.

'Nothing!' thundered Hades. 'Nothing!'

'Wait,' said Hilda. 'Let's click back several frames. Now look there. See that?'

'Yes. It's Mickey Mouse.'

'But look closely. What's he doing.'

'He's doing cartwheels between the crashing Dumbos

and exploding flares.'

'Exactly. And why is he doing that?'

'Because he's Mickey Mouse and that's Disneyland. Mickey Mouse just does stuff like that. Totally pointless and not even a little bit fun unless you are an imbecile who's totally blissed out on TV and junk food.'

'Look again. Mickey seems to be wearing leopard print trunks.'

'Good Lord! So he is. Whatever can it mean?'

31

Zip.

The light was dim, but compared to the absolute black inside the bag it was bright and welcoming as a summer day. There was a figure standing over her, a shadow among the shadows. There was no sense of threat and no drool dribbling on her, so it wasn't Maul. There was no sense of impending death by ice so it wasn't Flay. In fact, the dark shape seemed to be Mickey Mouse.

'Are you OK?'

She knew that voice and it didn't belong to Mickey.

Mickey Mouse took his own head off, a stray flock of photons hit the mystery figure and she saw: it was Timothy Adonis; Timmy, her personal assistant.

'Timmy!'

'Hi!' A big, goofy smile.

'But you're dead!'

'Am I? Cripes! That's a bit of a blow. I thought I'd dodged all the shooting. What do you think I should do?'

'Did you just rescue me?'

Timmy looked puzzled. Not for the first time in his life.

'I hope so. That's what I was trying to do.'

'Brilliant!'

'You just used that word again. I still don't get it.'

'You are brilliant! Oh, thank you, thank you, thank you!'

'Don't thank me, Victoria. We haven't got away yet. We're still under Disneyland and we've a long way to go. Are you able to run or shall I carry you in a heroic and muscular sort of way.'

'Oh, the heroic and muscular carrying does sound rather good, but after so long in that bag, I think I would like to use my own body before I forget how.'

'Let's get going.'

They were underground, in dark, echoing, fantasy of city planners and civil engineers. Victoria could see she was in a perfectly spherical concrete cavern, and this cavern was linked to others by perfectly tubular concrete canals, each of a bore that would accommodate much of Paris's rush hour traffic. In the spookily dim electric light, the water in the caves cast unstill reflections on the walls that would have been psychedelic had they not been so completely green. They were in a boat, a long, elegant boat with raised stem and stern . It was a gondola. Timmy grabbed the pole in a manly, in-charge sort of way and they were off, punting through the underside of Paris.

The kilometres, like the time, slipped beneath the keel of the gondola. Victoria kept an anxious eye for pursuit, but they were alone but for the dancing reflections and the gentle gush of sewage.

Shortly, the concrete gave way to walls of rock and earth as the modern tunnels serving the newer suburbs gave way to the ancient labyrinth beneath the city, Paris's subterranean other self, the one that through the ages has spawned mystery in its dark twists and turns. The rock and earth gave way to racks of skulls. Bats fluttered alarmingly overhead and tried energetically to get in Victoria's hair. Basilisks roiled and cavorted in the water. An arrowed sign dangled brokenly from a pole pointing to the centre of the Earth.

'Where are we?' asked Victoria, quite alarmed. She felt she had been released from captivity into the outer ring of Hell.

'The catacombs of Paris.'

'Oh. That's nice.'

'Not really, but they have fewer traffic lights than the road and fewer changes than the train.'

They passed an arch through which warm light glowed. Beyond the arch there was a cavern, opulently appointed. At the far end was a cinema screen showing a man and a woman sitting inside an open grave smoking cigarettes and not saying much. The cavern was filled with men and women in turtleneck sweaters who were smoking as much as the people on the screen and eating canapés and drinking wine.

'Oh, look, an underground art house cinema. I wonder what's showing. I wish we had time to stop for just one vol-au-vent. I do like a vol-au-vent, even *in extremis*.'

'Where we are going, you shall have all the vol-au-vent you want.'

Where they were going, once they had moored the gondola and climbed a long, spiral staircase back to ground level, was a forest in the outskirts of Paris. They had crossed the entire city underground. In the forest, in a convenient little clearing was a huge hot-air balloon, decorated in royal blue and a gold fleur de lis, the latest style for balloons in the mid 19th century.

'Voila!' exclaimed Timmy. 'Vos vol-au-vent.'

'Really, Timmy, you should see a doctor about those puns.'

They climbed into the balloon and Timmy cast off by slashing the tethering ropes with a swashbuckling sword.

The balloon rose into the early evening Paris air — a big bowl of blue against the even bluer bowl of the sky.

Paris sprawled below like a rather fantastic city sprawling beneath an improbable bag of hot air.

They could see the places that made defined Paris: the Eiffel Tower, the Champs Elysee, L'Arc de Triomphe, the Seine, Notre Dame cathedral and, eventually, Disneyland.

'We've just gone back the way we came,' remarked Victoria.

'No, we haven't,' protested Timmy. 'We just came under Paris through the catacombs in a boat. Now we are going over Paris in a balloon. Completely different ways of coming and going. We needed to get to a forest for the balloon. The alternative would have been taking the A4 to Rheims, and turning off in the outskirts for Ay or Épernay or the wonderfully named Bouzy, which would have been the way we were going and provided a forest, but what do you prefer, a dramatic punt under the old city or a mini-cab on a naff main road?'

'We could have taken the A4 south, switched to the A105 and then the A5 and the E54 to Sens, and then the E511 to Troyes and on to, say, Piney. The forest there has a rather attractive lake.'

'Too many E numbers. I have to watch my intake of artificial chemicals on top of the steroids. Besides, have you tried punting on a main road?'

'Silly me.'

Night blackened the sky and lit up the ground. The view was entrancing.

'Reminds me of It's a Small World,' said Timmy.

'Not quite as convincing.'

'It's going to get cold. I have some blankets and some food.'

They snuggled under heavy blankets together and Timmy passed Victoria a thermos that turned out to contain rich onion soup. He popped open a hamper and offered French bread, camembert, roquefort, tapenade, a dozen kinds of pâté, jambon, chicken confit, humus, oil-cured olives with herbs and feta, and a bottle of Bordeaux.

'Emergency rations,' he explained.

'What's the emergency?'

'Not eating it all.'

'What are you having?' asked Victoria.

'I have a pot noodle.'

The balloon drifted on through the night. The pair snuggled under the blankets sharing each other's warmth.

'But Timmy, I thought you were dead. I saw you go over the edge of the terrace when Maul said boo to you. How ever did you survive?'

'It was a close thing. That boo only just missed me. I thought I was a goner there for a moment or two.'

'So how did you survive the fall?'

'Well, I was really lucky. The rocks cushioned my fall and I wasn't hurt at all.'

'Gosh. Rocks. That is lucky.'

'And then I hid in a whirlpool at the foot of the cliff so that Maul and Flay would be able to see me.'

'A whirlpool! Well that gave those thugs a spin for their money. And then how did you manage to find me and rescue me in Disneyland?'

'Oh, that was easy. After I climbed up the sheer cliff face back to Villa Parque you and the kidnappers were already gone. But I did notice this horrible smell about the place.'

'Oh, yes, I noticed that. In fact, I was locked in the boot of the car with it. It was the kind of smell that would make grown tracker dogs cry and play dead without having to pretend.'

'That's the one! Well, I sort of howled and snuffled and followed that smell to the farm where you were being held captive.'

'And then,' exclaimed Victoria at the romance and adventure of it, forgetting for a moment the horror, 'you burst into the farmhouse, slew the fiendish plotters and bravely rescued me!'

'Er, no,' said Timmy carefully, thinking about this bit of the story. 'I don't believe I rescued you at that point.'

'Oh, no, you didn't. You just did that bit at Disneyland. Silly me. So why didn't you rescue me right away?'

'Erm. You weren't there. You'd gone.'

'Oh, what rotten luck.'

'But your father was there.'

'My father?'

'Yes, your father. And the world's press. All of it.'

'But what was he doing there? What was the world's press doing there?'

'He was apparently rescuing you. And the world's press was apparently making him smell of roses. Which is a pretty weird thing to do if I think about it.'

'Don't think about it, then, Timmy. But I don't

remember my father being there. I remember a washing machine and a dartboard, but I don't remember my father.'

'Ah, the thing is, you'd already gone, hadn't you.'

'Oh, of course. You are clever, Timmy. So what happened next? Did you rescue my father or did he rescue you?'

'Well, no one seemed to know where you were, so I followed your father back to his hotel, where I hid in the bathroom disguised as a Greek statue. That way, I was able to hear your parents discussing the exchange at 4pm in Disneyland. After that, it was a simple matter of getting from Monaco to Paris in a trice and arranging a hot air balloon, a subterranean gondola, some smoke bombs, and a fake Mickey head before the meeting.'

Moonlight and stardust glittered in Timmy's hair, which was being tousled by the velvety summer breeze. Space and all its stars and the earth and all its little lights wrapped them in romance.

'Oh, Timmy, you are clever. And brave.'

Sigh.

'Oh, it was all my pleasure,' said Timmy.

'You know, Timmy, all that has happened in the last few days seems to be changing me in some way — something deep down. The things that were recently so important to me like Atlantic City and Las Vegas and the Cayman Islands and fast cars, and unicorns, and spaceships, and an exciting life, and more unicorns and new bicycles and having the moon and white elephants and electroshock therapy and fame and nice holidays away from the pressures of being rich don't seem so important to me. Why is that? Even attention seems pretty much beside the point, whatever the point is.

But love seems more exciting and important than ever. Timmy, I think my things beginning with p are changing.'

'Plimsolls? Pies? Pantaloons?'

'No — oh, Timmy, how exciting! I even know what the p word is that I'm looking for. It's priorities. I think my priorities are changing. On top of it all, I seem to be able to count more than six. My hair is less blond and looking more brunette. Do you think this is growing up?' she asked breathlessly.

'Parrots? Purple? Pots?'

In the magic of the moment, Victoria failed to wonder that Timmy had spirited her away on the cusp of rescue by her father and mother.

32

Victoria was born into money — a very big, very literal, pile of it.

Her father, Hades Gousset, had decreed that his child should begin her life in the means in which he expected her to live it: rolling in dosh. This was to be in absolute contrast to the way in which Hades had begun his own life rolling in a ditch in Essex.

As his progeny gestated within her mother, Hades bought up all the best private clinics he could find, and then of those selected one. He had the rejected clinics demolished to ensure maximum exclusivity. He then closed the clinic to all admissions other than his wife and installed piles and piles of money in place of furniture. He would have done away with the delivery bed too but the staff convinced him it was useful for, you know, delivering babies such as his own, which was the whole point of the place, after all. He merely covered the birthing bed in bank notes instead.

And thus it was on the night of the birth, that with one last push — the final of just the two or three that constituted the whole of her labour — Persephone, a lady of unreasonable strength, ejected the baby Victoria, straight through the hands of a surprised midwife and into a commodious pile of £50 notes.

Hades, despite the reservations of Persephone, who still at some level believed in reality, proceeded to see to it that Victoria had exactly the kind of upbringing that he hadn't had and in the end gave Victoria a kind of upbringing that no one ever, anywhere on the planet, had ever had.

The sons of tsars, the daughters of kings, the children

of emperors, the offspring of presidents, the pop-outs of plutocrats, none had seen such pandering or cosseting or cocooning; such wealth, such spoiling, such lavishing, care and indulgence. The richest children in history looked like waifs and paupers compared to Victoria.

She went to a private girl's school in Switzerland, one that, like the clinic in which she was born, had been purged of its occupants and was exclusively hers, with a full staff and a school kitchen that would have been Michelin starred if anyone had been allowed in to find out about the food.

She had her own playhouse, known to the rest of the world as Versailles. Lambs gambolled on her eiderdown.

Where other girls had a pony, Victoria had the Spanish Riding School in Vienna, home of the high-stepping Lipizzaners.

Where other girls had dolls, Victoria had a modelling agency and a designer of haute couture that worked exclusively for her.

Victoria would want for nothing, and having known nothing else, there was nothing she particularly wanted.

One day, commuting between Geneva and London in her double-stretched flying limo, something just beyond the window caught Victoria's eye.

'What's that, Nanny?' she asked her nanny.

'That, Miss Victoria, is the actual world,' said Nanny carelessly. Horror crushed the woman's face at the realisation of what she had just said.

'If that's the actual world, Nanny, then where do I live?'

It was a question that came to define Victoria's life.

Nanny meanwhile, was quietly condemned to the rhubarb patch, and, in an effort to limit the damage, Hades built ever higher walls around his daughter.

33

With dawn, the vista had changed to mountains — dramatic white pinnacles of snow and ice.

Timmy heated the sphere of air above them less often and they drifted down to the level of the alpine peaks.

The winds were kind and about lunchtime Victoria spotted a castle perched sublimely on one of the mountaintops. They were headed right for it.

The castle was all towers and spires and turrets and spiky elegance and there was no discernible way up or down from it, no road or stairs or escalator or Sherpa.

With a skill not easily imaginable for a hunk who dressed only in leopard print trunks and the occasional Mickey Mouse head, Timmy guided the balloon to the ramparts of the tallest tower of the castle.

The couple stepped lightly from the basket to the battlements. Timmy plucked a hairgrip from Victoria's head and stabbed it into the side of the slowly sinking balloon, which went pllllllllllllllllllllllllllllugh between the peaks in a westerly direction before disappearing completely.

'Welcome,' said Timmy, to Schloss Himmel. Castle Heaven. My distant ancestor Count Backwards wanted to call it Schloss Shangri-la but no one could pronounce Schloss Shangri-la after a glass of schnapps, so Schloss Himmel it was.'

'Well, that's a perfectly perfect name. What happens next?'

'You fall in love with me, just as I have done with you, and we live happily ever after. That's what happens next.'

34

'There's only one person I know who wears leopard print trunks in the middle of a violent confrontation without any embarrassment,' said Sir Hades Gousset.

'Quite,' said Hilda Titanium. 'And I was under the impression that Maul and Flay had killed him.'

Hades and Hilda were still in the Porton Down bunker, huddled around a computer where they had been playing and replaying the Disneyland video until all the ones and zeros were rubbing off the hard drive.

'Maybe Maul and Flay can tell us something. After so long with our rainbow-drooling friends, they might be in the mood for a chat.'

When Hades arrived at the interrogation room, he found the supposed interrogators all sitting cross-legged on the floor in a big circle around the empty tables where interrogatees had formerly been.

'And where are Maul and Flay?' Demanded Hades.

'They went out to score, man,' he was told with a sense of awe.

And with more awe: 'They said they knew where to get some fairy dust.'

'And some fairies to go with it.'

'And some tabs with Pokemon prints on them.'

'And if you stare at them long enough, the Pokemon, like, talk to you, yeah?'

'Oh, bugger,' said Hades. 'And oh buggery bugger-bags.'

35

Persephone, back at the enormous rambling chez-Gousset home, clicked off her phone. She had been talking with the president of the United States of America who had agreed to the immediate mobilisation of his entire armed forces to hunt for Victoria. Persephone imagined the leaders of Britain, France, Germany, Italy, Spain, Holland, Denmark, Sweden, Portugal had already given him the heads up after she had enlisted their help. They had all been quite willing. This was the family of Hades Gousset, the most important man in the world they were dealing with. Some of the countries outside the western sphere of influence had been a mite sceptical. China, for example, had been tough to convince. They had wondered, bafflingly, what was in it for them, but Persephone had pointed out that with the largest population in the world they were in more need of underpants than anyone else, and Chairman Ping or whatever his name was had come round eventually. In the case of Russia, well, she had the photos, so persuading them had been a doddle.

Now to mobilise Canada, central and eastern Europe before a nice cup of napalm, and then she could get on with South America, Africa and the rest of Asia.

36

Life in Schloss Himmel was simultaneously idyllic and awful. It was idyllic because Schloss Himmel was a fantasy castle perched on top of an Alpine peak, and awful because Schloss Himmel was a fantasy castle perched on top of an Alpine peak and contained the adoring Timothy Adonis who wouldn't leave Victoria alone. It was also awful because there was no apparent way down the mountain and escape from Timmy's adoration.

Victoria and Timmy were in the extravagant main hall of Schloss Himmel, basking in the heat and luxury of a massive open fire, and wrapped in expansively furry animal skins. The furs were real and had an animal head at each corner to confirm their authenticity. Victoria's had the heads of an ibex, a bear, a mammoth and a coelacanth. Timmy's had the heads of a wolf, an eagle, an elk and a prehistoric human recovered from a neighbouring glacier. Within arm's reach there were open bottles of venerable and distinguished wine from the castle's venerable and distinguished cellar, and plates with finely cut slices of venerable and distinguished jamon that had been hanging in the venerable and distinguished pantry for nearly two centuries and which was now quite mature.

All the fur and embracing firelight made this the perfect place to make love.

'Oh, please fall in love with me, Victoria. Look I've

brought you a present from the mountain.'

'Oh. A frozen dead rabbit. How thoughtful. I'll put it with the frozen dead ptarmigan, the exotically yellow snow, and the scrapings of lichen you brought me earlier.'

'The mountain is bountiful with gifts.'

'Yeah, right.'

She unfurled herself from the vast fur she was wrapped in and threw another log on the fire just to distract herself and avoid Timmy's intense and unwavering stare.

'Oh, why won't you fall in love with me, Victoria?'

'People just don't fall in love to order, Timmy. Life isn't like that.'

'Why isn't life like that?'

'I don't know. Life just isn't like that.'

'Why don't you know why life isn't like that?'

'I don't know why I don't know why life isn't like that. That's just the way it is.'

'Why is that just the way it is?'

She resisted the urge to launch the next log at Timmy's face.

'You seemed to like me before,' said Timmy. 'You always wanted me around. You always made me come in the shower with you even when I wasn't dirty.'

'Yes, I did — do — like you, Timmy. But things have changed. I have spent a number of days in a bag. I've been to Disneyland. I'm turning brunette. Experiences like those change your outlook on life. I was young and idealistic and naive before all that happened. I'm more ... more ... more pissed off and traumatised now.'

'I don't understand. Surely you appreciate more deeply the important things in life like, er, love and beauty and, er, life.'

'Yes, Timmy. That's true.' It was time to be brutally honest. 'Look, Timmy, what I felt for you before was not love. It was bare, naked lust.'

'Lust. There you go using big words again. What is this "lust"?'

'Lust. I just wanted to shag your brains out.'

'Shag? Like a carpet?'

'No, shag like a rabbit. A very, extremely naughty and randy rabbit.'

'I had a rabbit once, but his name wasn't Randy. His name was Bambi.'

'Bang. Like a barn door in a gale.'

'Gail's a nice name for a rabbit. I wouldn't call a pet Bang, though.'

'You're really not with me, are you Timmy.'

'Oh, you're quite wrong there. I'm with you for ever and ever and ever.'

'Look. Tomorrow, let's just go down the mountain and go home. My parents are completely bonkers, but I'd quite like to see them now.'

'Oh, we can't do that. Not until you have learned to love me.'

'What?'

'I said, "Oh, we can't do that. Not until you have learned to love me".'

'No, Timmy. I'm afraid we have to go back down the mountain at first light tomorrow so that I can go back to my life.'

'Your life is here with me, now. I decided that. Besides, there is no way down the mountain. This place was made to be completely safe with no way in or out, which means no way in or out.'

'So what happened to the people who made it?'

'Oh they had to run away and leave the country when the local council realised they didn't have planning permission and set the zoning inquisition on them. In fact, that's how I came about. They fled to Croydon and made Adonises instead.'

'So, when you say there's no way in or out, how do you get in or out.'

'By hot air balloon, airship or helicopter.'

'And you have a hot air balloon, airship or helicopter stashed here.'

'Not at all. The place hasn't been used in two hundred years. The balloon we arrived on went west.'

'You mean I'm trapped here.'

'No, you have the freedom to go wherever you please in the castle and you can have as many frozen rabbits as you like.'

'You mean you're holding me here against my will?'

'Who's Will? Is he another rabbit?'

'You mean, I've been fucking kidnapped? Again?'

37

Persephone, sucking thoughtfully on her tumbler of napalm reflected that it might not have been a good idea to call the Dear Leader of North Korea, Kim Young-un, for help. He had sounded a bit too interested and had kept asking odd questions about what kind of underpants Victoria was wearing.

Oh dear.

38

The US special forces helicopter was as black as the night and just as silent. It skimmed over the Alpine peaks like an ethereal wraith, invisible to radar as it carried its cargo of human weapons to whatever secret location for a dramatic operation that no one would ever hear of and which might have involved rescuing Victoria, had it not just flown obliviously past her.

The North Korean helicopter, by contrast, clattered like a cutlery factory with Tourette's syndrome, waking up the entire population of Switzerland while it got lost trying to find Schloss Himmel. The radar of every European nation was tracking the helicopter, but because it was North Korean, Nato's personnel just slapped their thighs and laughed until they snotted themselves.

39

'What the banana cake is that?' worried Timmy as the castle shook around them.

'Sounds like a North Korean special forces helicopter,' said Victoria. 'I'm getting an awful feeling of oh no, here we go again. We have to get out of here. Timmy, there has got to be a way down the mountain.'

'Well,' said Timmy carefully. 'Not really.'

'Not really is not an absolute. How do we get down?'

'Well there's always the luge thing.'

'The luge thing. On a sheer rock face, without a luge track and with heavily armed North Korean agents chasing us?'

'Erm. Is yes, the right answer?'

'Yes.'

'Is that a yes?'

'Let's go.'

'But what if they say boo?'

There was a rapid thudding noise on the roof and a scream as the North Korean commandos deployed from the helicopter by fast rope. They didn't have a budget for ropes so they improvised by deploying by fast empty space.

Victoria and Timmy fled down the expansive stone staircase and through the cathedral-like hall to the broom cupboard under the stairs.

'What are we doing here?'

'Looking for Harry Potter.'

'Stop this all this whinging.'

'It was only a little whinging.'

They wedged into the narrow space together, their bodies pressed close.

'Honestly, Timmy, after all the opportunities you've had, I really don't think this is the — oh!'

Timmy yanked on a coat hook and the floor opened beneath their feet dropping them into a secret tunnel.

They landed, with a loud clang on some kind of metal cylinder.

'Wriggle,' commanded Timmy.

'Look, Timmy, we are way beyond that point —'

'It's the luge. You have to wriggle to get inside. Don't you watch the winter sports shows? Everyone wears Lycra, you know.'

'Oh. I see.'

The pair of them wriggled into the two-person luge.

As they worked themselves into the contraption, Victoria was able to make out that they seemed to be in some kind of cavity between floors or inside the walls of the castle. Perhaps some kind of secret escape route, or perhaps just a very compact garage space for a luge. It was also another dark unwelcome space and she had experienced far too many such spaces lately.

'Hold on tight,' said Timmy.

'I've never been in one of these things in my life. What do I do?'

'I've never been in one of these things before either, but I do like Lycra. I think the trick is to lay back, roll with me and keep all your parts inside the luge at all times so they don't get smashed off. Here goes.'

A trap opened in the floor, dropping them onto a chute, which sped them at an alarming downward angle towards the outer wall of the castle.

'Whoooooooaaaaaaaaaaagh!' screamed Victoria and Timmy together in perfect luge-team coordination. They hurtled toward the wall, which must have been nine thick metres of solid basalt. Victoria braced herself, ready to be spattered over the inside of the battlements. But the wall contained another cunningly concealed trap door and suddenly the luge shot into a blinding icy whiteness.

40

Victoria and Timmy might have made a silent and effective escape but for two things.

One of the two things was five foot six and extremely hungry. He was corporal Kim Ill-feeling of the 1st Extremely Supreme Commando brigade of the DPRK and was patrolling high on the ramparts of Schloss Himmel.

While his colleagues plunged mercilessly and effectively into the bowels of the castle — as per protocols directed by the Gloriously, Wonderfully, Supremely Dear Leader — Kim was fulfilling his sacred task of watching their behinds, and he was doing this by prowling the castle ramparts in a professionally alert and battle-ready manner. While his mind was wholly and supremely on the job in hand, a small lump of his consciousness not needed for his exalted task was whiling its time with noting the view.

This was his first time in the Alps. This was his first time out of North Korea. He couldn't help but noticing that the Alps had mountains. Lots of them, buttressing the sky in every direction he looked. They may have been very tall and dazzling but, he thought patriotically, they were not a patch on the incomparable and glorious mountains of his homeland which were gloriously, incomparably dumpy and brown and denuded of anything edible or that could be used for fuel.

This same unemployed part of his mind also noted how

hungry he was. He hadn't had a proper square meal since ... since ... well, not since he was born, if he thought about it.

In his home country, food was considered a counter-revolutionary decadence and eating was an irrelevance compared to the overarching task of keeping the ruling dynasty in as much opulence as possible. The ruling dynasty, the Kim family, were the definition of revolutionary purity and self-sacrifice and were therefore entitled to hog all the food the population could scrape from the thin soil.

It was ordained thus by the imperative of historical class struggle. It was also ordained thus by the unicorns.

Corporal Kim Ill-feeling had the same family name as his Glorious Leader. Kim Young-un was the father of the nation so it wasn't possible to have any other family name.

It was this idling part of Kim's mind that spotted something green. He froze. Green could mean only one thing: something potentially edible. Generally, the only exception to the Green is Edible rule was green paint, but Kim had occasionally eaten that too just in case.

Green might mean a cabbage or a bamboo shoot. It might mean leaves or grass or weeds. It might mean mould, but green implied photosynthesis and therefore probably meant nutrients in some form.

In this case the green was a bit off-green and meant lichen encrusting the crenellations of the castle top.

Kim quickly cast his eyes over the battlements and turrets of the castle to make sure no one was looking and then fixed his mouth to the cold stone and the lichen and began to suck.

His meal was interrupted almost immediately.

From far below, near the castle's base there was a clang and something like a torpedo shot out from the castle wall at great speed, sailed about twenty metres and went whump into the snow.

Kim, still mouthing the cold stone, wondered whether this was something he could ignore. He hoped it was something he could ignore. He felt that he was close to getting something out of the lichen and was most reluctant to pay any attention to whatever it was that just happened down below.

A torpedo was a torpedo, right? Nothing to get excited about. Usually we use them in the ocean but right now some twonk had decided he knew better and used one on a mountain. No big deal. This place was full of reactionary pigs and capitalist dogs and firing torpedoes on mountaintops is exactly the kind of dumb, inferior thing that capitalist pigs and reactionary dogs do. Ha! And the torpedo was going away from his helicopter, not towards it, so whatever, OK?

He summoned a mental image of running to his commanding officer and exclaiming, "Permission to report, sir, we are not under attack by a torpedo on a mountain, sir!"

"Very good, corporal Kim. Have this medal and get back to sucking lichen."

No, really, torpedoes were a one-way ticket to the re-education camp.

He sighed.

Two people had just got out of the torpedo. One was a god-like creature clad only in leopard print trunks and the other was a blond-ish, brunette-ish woman clad in lumpen, grey sweats.

He sighed again and bid farewell to the spit-soaked lichen. He very much regretted he had real reason to raise the alarm.

41

The second thing that foiled the silent and swift escape of Victoria and Timmy was a couple of hundred years old and completely mad. It was Count Backward — Otto — who had built Schloss Himmel, and who was a distant forbear of Timothy Adonis. It was Otto who had specified the luge in the design of the castle when it was originally built. He was not a specially sporting person, being riddled from birth with hereditary gout, and otherwise being haemophiliac and generally frail and cretinous as any fully paid-up member of the aristocracy had to be in those days. He had the luge installed because he had a love-hate relationship with altitude. He loved heights. He loved being king of the castle. He loved the dramatic vistas afforded by mountaintops. He hated clouds. He was pants-ruiningly petrified of clouds and clouds had a terrifying habit of hanging around mountaintops.

Clouds inspired in Count Otto Backward abject terror. Those big white fluffy things in the sky could inspire screaming, pants-wetting, hide-under-the-bed panic. The bigger, the whiter, the fluffier the cloud, the more Otto's underpants would suffer. Small, wispy clouds were no better because he thought they might get caught in his hair or that they might hide on top of the wardrobe in his room ready to pounce on him in the night.

The fear stemmed from a conviction that as a child he had once been eaten by a cloud.

One morning he was taking a health-imparting walk in the expansive grounds of the family mansion in an unusually thick pea soup of a fog. He asked his nanny what this curious opaque air was. Fog, he was told, was a cloud that had bumped into the ground. Otto enjoyed the novel thought that he was walking inside a cloud until he became separated from his minders and carers and became thoroughly lost and disoriented.

The fog was so thick that he could barely see his hand in front of his face, and what he could make out of his appendages was pale and ghostly and wraithlike. He assumed he was becoming one with the fog. He became convinced he was being digested.

His nanny quickly located him by his blood-curdling screams and rushed him back to the safety of the mansion, where demonstrations that he was, in fact, whole and unharmed did nothing to dissuade the young Otto of the thing his terror had convinced him of. Even at that young age Otto was aware that he was an heir to vast amounts of wealth and power and that reality was pretty well whatever he told it to be and so the being-eaten-by-a-cloud incident became official Backward history. If any of his nannies or minders or carers or doctors or teachers so much as sniggered at the story he would demand of his parents that they be fired. Fired from the cannons on the roof of the mansion. The labour laws of the day permitted — nay, demanded — such things.

Otto and his parents were from that day able to attribute his aristocratic frailty and haemophilia to the effects of being partially digested by a bank of water vapour rather than to generations of family inbreeding — his parents were brother and sister once removed — causing his DNA to disintegrate.

His family commissioned the most innovative designers of the day to create cloud-proof clothes. He wore hats with extravagantly wide brims to which were attached tubular spectacles that narrowed his field of view, reducing the chance of accidentally glimpsing his sky-borne nemeses. Wherever he went, flunkies would erect vast awnings to further reduce the chance of encounters and scurry around him with parasols the size of tents.

On foggy days when the clouds came down to personally get him, he would hide in a panic room in the heart of the mansion surrounded by armed guards and flaming braziers.

On cloudless days, lookouts would be posted on the roof of the mansion with telescopes to warn of the sudden approach of any white fluffiness. It was on days such as this and under heavy armed guard that Otto Backward discovered his love of heights and mountains. Tall places were the physical expression of his place in the world, towering above ordinary people and making up history as he went along.

When he announced that he was going to build an entire schloss on the tallest mountain possible in order to consolidate his loftiness once and for all, and especially for posterity, his retinue pointed out that this ambition might be considered a tiny bit incompatible with his nephophobia; that his fear of clouds might be at odds with his plan to live among them. Nonsense, he responded. He would line the castle walls with cannon to shoot down any clouds that got anywhere near. He would build fantastic airships from which clouds could be lassoed and towed away. For one as exulted and addled as he, nothing was impossible.

And just in case any sneaky little cloud did get past the lassos and guns, there would be the luge for fast escape. In his mind, nothing could get down a mountain faster than a luge. And so it was decreed that a luge should be included in the castle, and the fact that the luge had not yet been invented was no deterrence.

Perhaps it was the lack of the prior existence of luges on the planet that prevented his engineers and advisers to spot a particular and fatal problem with the plan. Or perhaps it was the fear of being shot out of a cannon that compelled them to keep their thoughts to themselves.

It was this problem that now stymied Victoria and Timmy in their bid to flee.

42

'Luge. Snow,' said Victoria. 'Not made for each other. Luges run on compacted ice, not deep and fluffy snow. We're lodged in this drift looking like a pair of complete twerps.'

'Oh, more banana cakes!' swore Timmy. 'We'll just have to use this emergency inflatable toboggan.'

He pulled a ripcord on his leopard print trunks and — poof! — there was an emergency inflatable toboggan for two. Timmy's trunks were a Hades Undies World product.

The appearance of the toboggan was not a moment too soon because at that moment, alerted by Kim Ill-feeling, the North Korean commandos had unpacked their jet-propelled snowmobiles and were giving chase.

Timmy and Victoria pushed off and hurtled down the near-sheer incline of the snowfield as the sleek, black snowmobiles launched from the towering ramparts of the castle above and thudded into the snow around the toboggan.

The engines of the snowmobiles roared.

The Korean machine guns went rat-a-tat.

'Switch machine guns from rat-a-tat to bullets,' the commander ordered. 'We'll take the cost of the bullets out of your salary next month, so be sure to get receipts from everyone you shoot.'

The emergency inflatable toboggan bearing Victoria

and Timmy slalomed between the trees as it flew to the bottom of the mountain.

Behind them came the black-clad commandos, two-up on their snowmobiles, one driving, the other shooting.

Bullets whined and pinged around Victoria and Timmy and tore chunks out of the pine trees. Timmy turned fast and tight among the trees and rocks. Suddenly there was a snowmobile right on their tale. The gunner levelled his gun at them and Timmy made an impossibly sharp swerve in front of a tree. The snowmobile and its riders failed to make the turn and went into the pine, which whipped back and catapulted machine and crew back up the mountain. Right away another snowmobile slotted in behind the hurtling trunks-cum-toboggan. Timmy tried the same sharp turn manoeuvre sending this one over an evil-looking black rock, to flail helplessly through the air and into the biggest, deepest snow drift in Europe.

Ahead of Timmy and Victoria, the side of the mountain seemed to disappear abruptly. There was a ravine and at the speed they were doing there was no way to avoid it.

'Ready?' shouted Timmy in the teeth of the slipstream.

'Ready,' confirmed Victoria. 'But for what?'

'On three. Three!'

'Whoooooooaaaaaaaaaaagh!' they screamed in perfect unison again.

The toboggan bounced over the lip of the ravine and buoyed on fantastic updrafts floated miraculously to the other side.

The hurtling snowmobiles were made of less buoyant, more gravity-afflicted materials than Timmy's trunks. One after the other they sailed into the air and disappeared among the trees that filled the ravine, each making an interesting voomp noise as it landed.

Victoria and Timmy swooshed on through the forest, elegantly twisting between the trees in the deep, comforting snow. Now free of the worry of their violent pursuers they could almost enjoy the ride.

The petrifying gradient became friendlier. They slowed down. And finally at the foot of the mountain, they skidded to a halt.

'We made it, Timmy! We made it!'

'Switch machine guns to menacing click mode.'

Click!
Click!
Click!
Click!
Click!
Click!

Click! went the machine guns in the hands of the North Korean commandos who were suddenly surrounding the toboggan.

'The ravine,' explained the commander. 'Shortcut. It was part of the plan all along.'

'Oh, buggery bugger-bags,' said Victoria.

'Hey, you with the pussy pants,' said the North Korean commander.

'Me?' asked Timmy.

'You,' said the officer. 'Boo!'

'Agh!' said Timmy and toppled over backwards in the snow with his legs in the air.

43

The North Korean helicopter clattered and wheezed its way from Schloss Himmel, traveling east — further east; further away from home and security. Victoria was jammed in between the stony-faced, black-clad commandos. No one spoke.

As far as Victoria knew, her parents had no idea where they were. As far as she knew Timmy was dead again. Timmy was as bonkers as her parents but he had saved her from Maul and Flay. It was a shame he hadn't saved her as far as the comfort of her own home and instead left her out on a limb where the North Koreans could get her. But his heart was in the right place. *Was* being the appropriate word, because his heart was now in a snowdrift in a dreadful Alpine place where a member of a royal family might run over it while skiing.

Night was falling. They were flying into the dark. She had no idea where.

The interior of the helicopter was cramped with commandos and their equipment. The craft shook and juddered and bounced through the air. The rats had to run really, really fast in their wheels to keep the rotor blades turning.

A commando appeared from the back of the helicopter with a tray on which tin mugs were precariously balanced and began distributing them — one to Victoria too. She couldn't help noticing that the mug was empty and wondered whether coffee or soup would be brought round separately in a thermos or kettle or pot, but, no — with alarm, she saw that the men were all pretending to drink from their similarly empty cups.

'Combat rations,' the commander told her. 'Designed by the Dear Leader himself. He is an expert nutritionist. This will keep my team at peak strength and endurance whatever happens. There is nothing the Dear Leader doesn't know everything about.' He glanced pensively at one of the rats in its wheel. 'Get it inside you. It may be basic but it's good stuff.'

Victoria thought, basic? You don't get more basic than an empty cup, that's for sure.

'I am Commander (non-supreme) Kim Il-bond of the Supreme Leader's Secret Service and these men are of the Supreme Leader's Supremely Special Forces here on supremely secret missions assigned personally by Our Dear, Darling Leader himself.'

Victoria made a point of looking supremely unimpressed.

'And you are Victoria Gousset, daughter of Sir Hades Gousset, underpants magnate, the richest, most powerful person in the world. Our Beloved Leader will be happy to receive you into his presence.'

'How do you know who I am? How did you know where to find me?' demanded Victoria.

'Military secret,' said the commander. 'The Dear Leader knows everything. Nothing is hidden from the Dear Leader.' He laughed like a man unused to laughing and who found the activity painful.

'Where are you taking me and why?'

'Ah. That is also a military secret. We have a good military. A supreme military. The best supreme military in the world. The most secrets, the best secrets. Supremely best secrets — which is itself a supreme secret but I told you anyway. I may have to shoot you now.'

'Oh, please, be my guest.'

'Thank you for the invitation, but I cannot shoot you yet. I cannot shoot a guest of Our Extreme Leader. The Dear Dearer Dearest Leader requires information from you. You must arrive in Pyongyang intact. You are most privileged.'

'The Dear Leader requires information from me? I

thought you said he knows everything. Whatever he wants to ask me, if he knows everything he must know the answer already.'

'The Dear Leader is indeed omniscient. Perhaps he wants to check that you know the answers.'

'By the same score, if he is omniscient, he already knows whether I know the answers.'

'Perhaps, then, he is testing your honesty by checking whether you give him the correct answers.'

'Same thing. If he is omniscient, he'll know in advance whether I am truthful or not.'

The commander went back to eyeing the rats.

'The ways and will of the Supremely Supreme Leader are not always clear to mere mortals like us. There is a time to accept, to trust and let his hand guide us in the grand scheme.'

One of the rats suddenly stopped running, stiffened and toppled over, its little paws clasped to its chest. The helicopter immediately lost speed and stability and began spinning and wobbling.

Commandos leapt to their feet and span the rat wheel by hand, shouting alarums and orders at each other. The helicopter stopped spinning and somehow clung to the air.

Keeping the rat wheel spinning without a rat was going to exhaust any human so commander Kim organised a rota to keep the rotors spinning — a rotor rota.

It was going to be a long night.

Kim gave some orders about the deceased rat, which was divided into a few small portions. The nose and whiskers, a delicacy, went to the pilot, to keep him from defecting mid flight. The legs went to NCOs by seniority and the commander, Kim Il-bond had the choicest part, the tail, which he sucked happily through the rest of the journey.

44

By dawn, the helicopter was in an entirely different part of the world. Instead of the snowy peaks or verdant green fields of Europe, Victoria could see barren, red mountains below. More than being another part of the world, it might have been another planet, a distant and forbidding planet; the kind of place sensible people didn't go without a huge, national aerospace agency backing them up; the kind of place in which, if misfortune or malice befell you, you would never be found.

Victoria didn't want to be there at all. She felt the furthest from home she had ever felt and was wondering whether she would ever find her way back.

'It's OK. We can go back now. The flight was very interesting and I am grateful to the Dear Leader for the experience but —'

'Oh, but we are going back, but not to where you came from. We are going back where we came from and you and your head full of secrets are coming with us. First —' the helicopter began to descend — 'we have to make a little stop to transact some business regarding nuclear weapons and to get a new rat.

45

The crew slid open the big side doors of the chopper. This might have been in readiness for landing or readiness for crashing or just to let some air in — whichever, the open doors afforded Victoria a fine view of their landing site, which was as improbable as the landscape. Their destination was clearly of the earth but not made by it; it was a thing, a place, a structure, if you like, clearly hewn of the rock by sentient hand, not by natural processes. Whose sentient hands and how many fingers they had, or from which part of the galaxy, was not immediately obvious because this hewn thing was not your everyday, common-all-garden hewn thing. This was a thing hewn by a sentience that had some pretty wacky, out-of-this-world ideas. It was not a sentience that had words like 'normal' or 'sensible' in its lexicon.

The structure was a mountain fortress but completely unlike the one Victoria had just left.

The towers, the walls, the keep, the whole body of this castle, was carved from the very mountain that it topped. While Schloss Himmel was all Alpine loveliness, this place was built by people in a very grim and austere frame of mind. This was something that could only have been built by people who had never heard of Disney or lederhosen. Massive slabs of granite that reared out of the desert floor as if propelled by some cataclysmic, angry-

God-related event were frozen in mid-leap for all eternity. Carved into this natural tower were battlements, walkways, windows, arrow slots — all the necessary trappings of a proper castle. The trained military eye would spot very quickly that there was no main gate, no main entrance at the ground level, which meant no weak point for an attacker to storm, which meant that this was definitely not a fortress you would want to fuck with.

In less gentle days this citadel would have kept out just about any uninvited visitors, who, on simply seeing the place would have gone home and taken up macrame rather than dash themselves futilely on its walls. In these kinder times it had pretty much the same effect.

Victoria hoped she and her fellow travellers were not the uninvited kind of guests.

The early morning sun poured gold on the red of the mountain and castle, and, in return, mystery and age poured out of the rock. Victoria felt conflicted by the majesty and beauty and obvious skill and tenacity of its building on the one hand, and on the other hand, the sheer implacable scariness of the place and the fact that she was there.

The helicopter touched down on the pinnacle of the castle with a tired scream and the crew took fire extinguishers the remaining rat, which was smouldering in its wheel.

Kim and his men clambered out and stretched their legs.

The hosts were there to greet them. Victoria again hoped they were hosts because they were clearly not people to disturb without a very good reason indeed. They were clad in loose linen outfits and rough turbans, all of which looked as if they had seen better days — had seen better centuries. Their faces were hidden inside unfeasibly large beards and their eyes had that far-away look that suggested they had stuff on their mind that was far too important for this paltry little reality. They carried large guns, possibly larger than the ones the North Korean commandos carried.

Victoria felt that there were altogether too many firearms for one rooftop meeting between two sets of intense people.

'Greetings from the Supreme Leader of the Democratic People's Republic of Korea, Supreme Nob of the Politburo, Supreme Commander of the Heroic People's Army, Supreme Guardian of the Pantry, Sexiest Man Alive, Converser with Unicorns, Father of the Nation's Children, Keeper of the Kimchi; Pooper of the Odourless Poop.'

One of the bearded men stepped forward and probed the visitors with a steely and piercing eye.

Victoria stood up in the doorway of the helicopter to get a better view of the spectacle.

Kim continued, 'Our One True Leader presents his fraternal and most respectful salutations to you and conveys his heartfelt wish that all our fruitful transactions are conducted with sincerity and an open spirit.'

The bearded man's eye fixed on Kim as if seeing him for the first time. He drew himself up proud straight.

'My title is Khodavande Alamut, Lord of Alamut. My name is — Whoa! Holy Mary Mother of God! What's that?' he screamed in a conspicuously Irish accent.

The hosts of Alamut fell into hubbub and raised their big guns at the North Koreans who raised their big guns back and went what? what? what? All of a sudden, everyone was in an armed standoff.

'A woman! In Alamut! How did she get in here?' demanded the lord of the castle through his unfeasible beard and even less feasible accent.

Victoria was still dressed in the grey baggies Flay had given her in France before stuffing her in a bag, but she was still very identifiably a woman. She was bathed in the golden glow from the sun. The gentle desert wind blew her blond-ish, brunette-ish hair across her face.

'She is with us. She is our prisoner,' explained Kim.

'Avert your eyes, brothers, unless you are aroused!' bellowed the leader of the hairy, baggy ones, with his hands and big gun held over his face as if fending off the

Hydra's gaze. His army of gunmen loyally followed suit, only some of them peaking between their fingers to get a proper ogle at their destruction.

'We are supremely taking this woman back to Korea with us,' Kim explained. 'Against her will,' he added with some satisfaction.

This news provoked the lord of Alamut to pause in his mythic struggle.

'She is not a free woman?'

'A hostage at my mercy.'

'Well, that's a bit better, I suppose. Let me confer with my brothers.' The beardy men got together in a big huddle. The conference was fairly succinct and the main order of business seemed to be rolling some tobacco mixed with a dark resin into a cigarette made with several cigarette papers, which was lit and passed around.

The leader of the hosts of Alamut reported back. 'She'll have to cover up. There's a danger of arousal if women don't cover up. She should, you know, wear a headscarf, at least. The hair especially should be covered up. You know what hair does to you. You just want to touch it all the time and put it in your mouth.'

'A headscarf? Woman, do you have a headscarf?'

'Yes, I have lots of headscarves. Lots and lots and lots of them.'

'Well put one on now.'

'I'm happy to. You can drop me off somewhere there's life I can catch a plane or even a train or a bus. The headscarves are all in my closet at home, you see.'

'You don't have one with you?'

Victoria flapped her clothes to demonstrate that all she had was what she was standing in.

The men of Alamut flinched and shuddered and covered their eyes again.

'Ouch! Don't do that!' The leader bellowed. 'What you really need is a full burqa. Are you sure you don't have one of those?'

'Check the equipment for a full burqa!' roared the commander.

After a moment: 'We don't have a full burqa, but we do have an empty one.'

'An empty burqa? What do you — That's not a burqa, that's a bucket. Look for something else.'

'No, no, that'll do,' interjected the Khodavande Alamut.

'The bucket will do?'

'Yeah, the bucket will do fine. If it covers the hair that's good. No one will get aroused at a bucket.'

'Put the bucket on her head!'

'You are not putting a bucket on my head!'

Clang!

'Ow!'

'Right. How about some refreshments? It's been a busy morning. We have some great cold tea and dried goat meat. And do you have the package?'

'Do you have a rat?'

46

'If we can't get you a rat here, we'll send out for one,' the big-bearded, be-turbaned head of the men of Alamut told the Korean commander, as if rats could be ordered like pizzas. 'Whatever — my main man Billy's on it.'

'It is bad news you don't have a rat to hand. We have a long way to go. Our Fantastically Glorious Leader will be discommoded if we are delayed.'

They were in a large hall or cavern at the rocky heart of the mountainous fortress. The morning sun angled majestically through high, arched windows and lit the place without need for electric lights, candles or torches. The air had a gentle smoky quality imparted by cooking fires in the hall over which tea was being made, and the several large, carrot-shaped cigarettes that were being passed around.

Everyone was sat on the luxuriantly carpeted floor in two long lines, facing each other, the commandos on one side, the turbaned and bearded men on the other — the commandos staring hungrily at the piled slices of dried goat on the platters between them and twitching with malnutrition.

The commander introduced himself.

'I am Commander (non-supreme) Kim Il-bond of the Supreme Leader's Secret Service and these men are of the Supreme Leader's Supremely Especially Special Forces, here on supremely secret missions assigned personally by Our Bumptious Leader himself.'

'I'm Seamus-i Sabbah, also known as the cool dude of the mountain. You may have heard of me.'

'Only from comic books.'

'And collectively we are the Hashishin. This is Billy, and that's Kenny, and Brian and well, the whole gang.

Collectively: 'Hi!'

'We're here on a religious retreat.' There was a giggle from his neighbour, Billy.

'I am honoured to meet you. Excuse my impertinence. I am something of a specialist in military history. I have heard of the Hashishin and the semi-legendary fortress of Alamut but weren't the Hashishin Shia Nizari Ismaili Muslims active in the 11th century, a section of the army assembled by Hassan-i Sabbah who unified the Nizari Ismaili state in a revolt against the corrupt Seljuq caliph?'

'That's us.'

'And weren't the Hashishin warriors specially trained in the arts of concealment and infiltration for the purposes of assassination? Rather like a middle-eastern ninja?'

'You know your lore, man.'

'Wasn't the order of the Hashishin defeated and dissolved in the thirteenth century by an invading Mongol army?'

The leader of the Hashishin gestured at his band of men. 'How dissolved do we look?'

'I know that the Hashishin tried to go underground at that point in history, but by the 15th century even the clandestine order had disappeared. It is incredible to think that you have actually survived as an organisation all these centuries and remained invisible.'

The chief Hashishin shrugged modestly. Billy, Kenny and Brian giggled immodestly.

There was more on Kim's mind. 'The English word assassin actually comes from the name Hashishin, doesn't it.'

'In one! Yeah. And they smoked a lot of hash. That's where the name Hashishin comes from. People who smoke hash.'

There was another giggle.

The commander was thoughtful a moment. 'But is it not the case that the Hashishin didn't actually smoke hash, that the drug taking was a myth, simply a term of insult dreamed up by their enemies? A bad name that stuck?'

'We've actually been known to partake of the odd toke.'

There were guffaws of laughter down the line of Hashishin.

'Muslims don't generally approve of drugs. Saying someone smokes hash is the equivalent in other countries of saying someone drinks window cleaner. Sorry, I don't mean to tell you your culture. I was just curious.'

'Ah, never mind. Have a bang on this number and cheer up. Look. The Hashishin are a bunch of highly skilled — oh, by the way, dig into the dried goat, lads. We've also got corn flakes for if you get the serious munchies. Where was I? Oh, yes, highly skilled assassins versed in the dark arts of whatever it was you said before. We're, we're, we're ... Billy, what's that word beginning with a?'

'Erm, ascetics, was it?'

'Ascetics. That's the bugger. We're ascetics, which means people who don't actually have to do anything because we have a higher porpoise. Purpose, not porpoise.'

Guffaws and splutters.

'And we smoke a lot of hash.'

Some of the Hashishin keeled over clutching their sides.

'And please forgive me again. But Seamus doesn't sound like a Nizari name either.'

'Nizari? Muslim? I don't know about any of that. I'm Catholic and I'm from Donegal.'

'I'm sorry, we were under orders from Our Gorgeous Leader to meet with a dangerous subversive organisation in order to disseminate secrets of nuclear fission and bomb making as part of a common purpose to bring the decadent and oppressive western governments and their proxies to their knees and impose a new world order based on rationality, austerity, hard work and no play. I seem to have the wrong address.'

'Oh, no, you have the right address. We are most definitely dangerous. This hash is a fucking killer. And we are most definitely hell bent on the destruction of the western way of life.'

'It is very commendable that you wish to destroy the western way of life. I can see why our Ultra-Amazing Leader has empathy and common purpose with you. But I am curious. You are of the western culture and yet you want to turn against the cradle of your upbringing. You are not only turning your back on everything you were taught to believe in but you want to raze it too. Can you explain this to me so I may understand and present it to the world as an inspiration?'

'It's very simple really. The world we in the west come from is very affluent and comfortable. But at what price to the spirit is all this materialism? Our countries are full of interesting restaurants and nice cafes where you can get a cappuccino whenever you want; on-tap health care, universal education, centrally-heated houses with hot and cold water, a ready supply of diverse and nourishing foods, music, theatre; social, intellectual and racial diversity — but who wants all that?'

'Quite,' said Kim, his stomach rumbling. 'The appearance of affluence is actually about enriching the few at the expense of the many.'

Seamus frowned. 'I don't know about any of that. You're getting a bit technical there for me. My point is that is all requires, you know, doing stuff. Getting out of bed, getting off the sofa and getting stuck in. We can't be bothered with any of that. Can we lads?' he asked of his comrades.

'Too right, Seamus,' they affirmed waving bits of goat and joints at him.

'And you have to wear a suit and a tie and, you know, be places at certain times. It's not for thinking people, that's for sure.'

'I'm not sure I follow,' confessed Kim. 'You are dedicated to the overthrow of the western way because ... you don't like to get out of bed?'

'And it's boring. Look, you have to have a job and be the same as everyone else and be interested in bloody insurance and wallpaper and the new corner store and the re-development of the docks into an arts and crafts centre, which is really institutionalising hippies. Boring, boring, boring. So, what do you want? Cafes and pubs and cinemas and security and nice houses — or a grim cave in an empty desert? It stands to reason, doesn't it. This way we get to hang out in a mountain-top fortress, calling ourselves Hashishin and smoking lots of the stuff and you can't beat that.'

Kim's English was very good but he wasn't sure he was understanding anything that Seamus was telling him. 'But why do you need nuclear technology?'

'Deterrence.'

'Deterrence?'

'Yeah, we're deterring people from hassling us and telling us to gets jobs and haircuts. And when we've done that, we'll deter them from these daft uptight lifestyles and not smoking tons of hash.' Everyone thinks dopers are losers. We're going to show them they're wrong on that point, and then we're going to spread the word. It's the end of bland western civilisation and the start of a fragrant, smoke-filled future. It's the end of the world as we know it and I feel fan-bloody-tastic.'

'OK. So there's no religious motivation. Why do you insist the woman's head be covered?'

'Look,' said Seamus conspiratorially, 'You've got twenty blokes here, a ton of hash and no magazines and no internet connection. You get women in here and it's going to be fucking arousals all over the place, and we can't be doing with that. These minds of these fellows are already fragile through asceticism and single-minded dedication to the cause. One whiff of oestrogen and there's going to be a mental pile up. There's going to be bits of psyche all over the place.'

It seemed to Kim that the psyches on show today were already pretty much all over the place.

'And let's face it,' Seamus continued, 'ninety-nine percent of all distraction from the life of peace and contemplation comes from women. Don't say it's not so. Who is it telling you get off the sofa? It's a mother, a sister, a girlfriend, a wife. Who is it telling you to get a job? Ditto. Who is it giving you grief in the JobCentre and cancelling your benefits? It's probably a woman behind the desk. Have you noticed how many women work in those places?'

No, Kim had not. He had never been in an Irish JobCentre. Where Kim came from no one lounged around on sofas. There were no sofas to lounge on. Where Kim came from, their grandparents had long-since burned their sofas to stave off icy death in the middle of the harsh winters. Where Kim came from people spent all their time scratching around for food and sucking up to The Party so they didn't end up in a re-education camp.

'It must be in the female DNA, all that caring about what other people are doing. And when they're not hassling you about the unimportant things in life they are driving you to distraction with their hair and lips and fragrance and hips and all that and how is a man supposed to concentrate on the deeper things in life with all that arousal going on? And when they've got you all in a state of amour, they tell you to fuck off and have a shower and get a life and they leave and how can a man concentrate on the ineffable with all those tears in his eyes?'

'So, there's no place for women in your brave new world.'

'Oh, no. They can make the tea and put the biscuits on the table and that, but under certain conditions. Silence and invisibility being two of those conditions. Or under a sheet.'

They glanced over at Victoria sitting outside the group of men. She had the bucket pushed up over her eyes and was testing some dried goat with her nose. Her nose evidently didn't like what it was finding out about the dried goat.

'And buckets help?'

'Buckets are a big help, yeah. Now. As to business. How about the package of stuff, the nuclear things you are supposed to be delivering me.'

'Ahh. The nuclear things I am supposed to be delivering to you. I'm just waiting on the decryption codes from Pyongyang. How about the rat?'

'Ah, the rat. I'm just waiting for Billy to stun one with a broom.'

Billy was sitting next to Seamus, smoking. He waved a broom at Kim and gave him a conspiratorial wink.

47

Seamus discovered the delights of doing nothing at an early age — possibly as early as the cradle.

He discovered the hell of being asked to do anything soon after. He has yet to discover the hell of actually doing have never ventured beyond the asked-to stage.

He only learned to walk, grudgingly, when he learned the ability facilitated doing nothing in a variety of ways: doing nothing on the sofa, doing nothing in the bog, doing nothing on the sofa after a walking trip to the fridge, doing nothing in bed, doing nothing in bed after a walking trip to the toilet because even Seamus was forced to admit that doing nothing in bed was far better than doing nothing in bed in a pool of his own excrement.

Later in his growing up he learned the pleasures of doing nothing in the park, to which he had to walk; doing nothing in the games arcade, the cafe and, later, the pub. Then there was doing nothing with his girlfriend, which lost him a lot of girlfriends. In his late teens he learned the ultimate doing nothing: doing nothing with a spliff. He needed walking skills to get around to arrange the hash and transport himself to a sofa or a bed or a carpeted floor or park bench or patch of weeds on some wasteland or a mildewed mattress in a derelict building or a queue in a JobCentre. Walking was as much as he would concede to doing.

It was at this time that he discovered the hell of people — especially women — insisting that he do something. Already noted the girlfriends that swiftly left as soon as his commitment to indolence became apparent. His mother had an energetic way of objecting to his life on the sofa.

There the sister, the one to whom he was always compared, a sister full of vim and get up and go who was always yelling at him to get up of the sofa and go out and get a job. Then the staff at the JobCentre always seemed to be women. Not shrill in the way his sister was, but scarily quiet and calm. They would look over their reading glasses at Seamus in a way that suggested they could see right inside his soul and every secret would be revealed to them and what they could see through the fog of hash was a great nothing punctuated by flashes of TV, corn flakes and masturbation.

The harping came not just from females. Authority was in on it too. The police, for example, would confiscate his stash whenever they could. They would arrest the people he bought from, leaving Seamus with famines and spells of haunting pubs and parks until he could find someone new to buy from. He was well known to the police. They didn't ever arrest him because they were aware that his purchase of prohibited substances was for personal use only, and that Seamus had no friends to sell to, anyway. Especially not female friends.

The police enjoyed their encounters with Seamus. Justifying stopping and searching him was never difficult to justify with probable cause because every time they stopped and searched him he was carrying something. The mere presence of Seamus was probable cause that he was carrying. The local constabulary was rarely without a little toke to go with their tea.

The other authority was the most terrifying one for a young man: his father.

Seamus senior was a workaholic and an abstainer. Seamus's father was a good father. He was a good provider, slow to anger, would attempt to communicate rather than lecture. He worked long hours at a company he part-owned. It was a sort of scientific job. Boffin's work. The company specialised in making artificial fibres and their main clients were something called NASA and something else that had a silly-but-scary name, like Hell's Underpants, or Hades Undies World, or something.

Whatever, Seamus senior was a massively dedicated to family and work. If Seamus junior had one tiny criticism of his father, it was his general reasonableness and unending humanity.

Seamus's father would come home from work — occasionally very late in the evening — and Seamus would be on the sofa in doing-nothing mode — or on the floor in doing-nothing mode, or upstairs in bed in doing-nothing mode, or absent-mindedly on the windowsill with the cat in doing-nothing mode. His father would look at him for a moment, silently — appraising perhaps — but without obvious judgement and then would try to make friendly conversation.

'Hello, Seamus. What kind of day have you had?' Or he'd try to talk about football or tell a joke or might offer help with anything at all.

And Seamus would reply 'Oh, you know,' or 'Brill,' or 'Whatever.'

Seamus's small criticism of his father was that his boundless good sense and humanity and lack of judgement made Seamus feel extremely — extremely — fucking guilty.

While the world got on with discovering the internet, social media, aspirations, sexuality and cappuccino, Seamus let it all go by. But he couldn't be happy because all the harping at him just went on and on. A small and irritating part of him felt, despite his best efforts to ignore and excise it, that he ought to do something about it but since doing wasn't his thing he found himself in a state of stalemate with himself and everything else.

Seamus got fed up of this.

Things came to a head one grisly, drizzly morning in February. Seamus was on his way to the JobCentre when he bumped into Hilary in the street. Seamus liked Hilary. She had long, dark brown hair, which today was pulled back in a lush ponytail. She had these deep-blue eyes that physically dazzled you. And she had this smile that that could launch you to the stars.

Seamus doted on Hilary from afar, but very much

wanted to dote on her from extremely, intimately close. When he saw Hilary this morning he stepped in front of her and stopped her in her tracks. He stared at her, trying to think of something to say.

'Look, fuck off, Seamus and get a wash. And just fucking ... do something with yourself.' And she strode off, with that lush ponytail swinging in the air behind her and her sapphire eyes looking right past him.

Seamus found in her place constables Leary and Keasey who rummaged in his pockets to extract what treats they could find.

'Have a nice day, Seamus,' they told him. 'Though ours is looking better than yours.'

Seamus plodded on to the JobCentre, where, while waiting his turn he extracted his reserve supply of psychotropic combustibles, which were secreted in a part of his body that most police officers didn't like to search. The staff of the JobCentre and the ladies and gentlemen waiting there had opinions about Seamus retrieving his stash from body cavities in public and the police were called. The responding officers were, of course, constables Leary and Keasey, who were more interested that Seamus had this backup — as it were — stash than the fact that he had attempted to retrieve it in a public place. They took the young man to the station to be searched properly by constable Kinsey, who was one of the few officers who actively enjoyed searching the locations other officers didn't like to know about.

Officer Kinsey found nothing to write a report about but he did suggest to Seamus that he got a fucking bath.

The officers then rang Seamus's family to ask whether they wanted the police to give Seamus a lift home, thus ensuring that his family knew where he had been during the day and why and what he had done.

The family declined the offer of a lift but Leary and Keasey dropped him off anyway ensuring that the whole neighbourhood saw him getting out of a police car and being escorted to his front door.

Seamus's mother and sister went ballistic at him but his

father just looked at him for a moment and then asked whether there was anything — *anything* — that he could do to help.

In that moment Seamus realised that if the world would not accommodate him, he would have to change the world so that it fucking did.

That same night, Seamus went on the road. While everyone slept, he filled his pockets and old school bag with anything he thought he might be able to sell — family heirlooms, ornaments, passports, computers, mobile phones, the lot — and he left.

In time, historians, Seamus thought, might criticise this move as actually being tantamount to doing something, but to Seamus it was a strategic doing nothing.

From then on, he travelled far and wide, seeking and gathering kindred spirits.

Seamus dreamed of an ideal society, one in which real men were free to be nothing, where hassling was against the law. And where women were unable to ever tell him to get his shit together or tell him to fuck off, no matter how sapphire their eyes might be.

Several months later in a palace in Shangri-la — actually a pub in Stoke Newington, but it may as well have been Shangri-la for all Seamus knew where he was — a stranger told him about the legendary, the historical Hashishin of Alamut and suddenly Seamus knew exactly what he should do.

48

'Come this way, Ms Gousset.'

Clang!

'You can remove the bucket in order to see your way through the door. In fact, you can leave it off until such time as we want you to put it back on while we beat it with a stick.'

'Thank you. I don't know why I'm saying thank you for letting me take off what you shouldn't have me wearing in the first place, or why I'm saying thank you to someone who has no business giving me orders, or why I'm saying thank you to someone who has carted me off from where I belong to who knows where against my will, or saying thank you to someone who said boo to Timmy in the snow.'

'You're welcome,' said Kim Il-bond. 'Please take a seat at this rude and wobbly dungeon table. It's so rude and wobbly, I believe the Hashishin may have acquired it from a British pub. Now, I will shine a desk lamp in your face. Standard interrogation procedure.'

'You haven't turned it on.'

'Well, there's no electricity at Alamut. We have to make do. And there are the pliers for your nails.'

'I don't have any wood, so I probably don't have any nails that need removing.'

'Finger nails, Ms Gousset.'

'Can I gulp?'

'It would be normal at this point.'

Victoria, Kim Il-bond and an escorting pair of commandos were in a very rough-hewn chamber off the main hall. The Hashishin remained in the hall, discussing the exact jurisprudential philosophy of the spliffate and what sort of wallpaper it should have, while manufacturing more joints for the glorious day when it came.

Kim's commandos kept a cautious eye on them with machine-guns, not that such caution was necessary. Being jumped by the Hashishin at this time would be as likely as being jumped by a heavily sedated sloth.

'What exactly is going on now?' she asked.

'I have received orders from Pyongyang to begin your interrogation even while we are here.'

'Save time later, I suppose.'

'Indeed. We have been unfortunately delayed in our journey by the shortage of one rat.'

'Odd. The place seems full of rats to me. Rats with guns.'

'The British are renowned for their humour. I can't see why.'

'Why exactly does this Pyongyang bloke want me? I can't say I've ever met him.'

'Pyongyang is the capital city of the Democratic People's Republic of Korea. It is where my superiors are located and from where I take orders.'

'I thought Raleigh was the capital.'

'Raleigh is the capital of North Carolina. Pyongyang is the capital of North Korea. Two different things. Now, to answer your question, my superiors have some urgent lines of enquiry they think you can help them with.'

With a flourish befitting a lace-cuffed magician on a prime-time variety show, Kim Il-bond slapped down a sheaf of printed images and spread them out in front of Victoria.

'Do you recognise these?'

Each of the images was of a pair of underpants — computer-generated 3D renderings, apparently right off the designer's hard drive.

'Where did you get these?'

'I am asking the questions.' Smugly, Kim turned to the guards and said, 'I have always wanted to say that.'

Turning back to Victoria, 'Just tell me whether you recognise these objects.'

'They're underpants.'

A guard hand-cranked a huge, ancient reel-to-reel tape recorder and Kim spoke into a microphone the size and appearance of the grille of a 1957 Corvette.

'Interview between Commander (non-supreme) Kim Il-bond of the Supreme Leader's Super-Secret Service, interviewing the prisoner purporting to be Victoria Gousset. Date: today. Location: the Fortress of Alamut.

'On presenting the prisoner with these images —' he pointed the microphone at the images '— she correctly identified them as underpants, thus irrefutably proving that she knows underpants when she sees them.'

'Could have been a lucky guess,' commented Victoria.

Kim covered the microphone with his hands. 'Let's assume for the moment you have offered irrefutable proof.'

Victoria shrugged.

Back to the microphone. 'Having established irrefutable proof, I proceed to the next question.

'What kind of underpants are these?

'I have just asked the subject what kind of underpants they are.'

'I don't think you need to tell the microphone what you just said. I think it was probably listening.'

'The answer to my question, please.'

'They're the kind of pants you wear under other things.'

'Can you be more specific?'

'The kind you wear around your loins.'

'Excellent. The subject has just identified the underpants as loin-hugging underpants worn under outer clothes. Now we are getting somewhere. The subject has not only demonstrated she knows what these images represent but what the purpose of the represented items is.'

'Or I just made some lucky guesses.'

Kim covered the microphone and poked his tongue out at Victoria.

Kim leaned in close. 'Now, can you tell me the brand and model of each?'

'Yes. Probably.'

'Ha! You see? Irrefutable proof that she subject claims to be able to tell me the brand and model of each,' Kim exclaimed into the microphone.

Silence.

'Go on then!'

'Oh. Well. The first is a pair of Snug-O-Pants, whose marketing point is that they are, well, snug. They come in one colour, grey, and two lines, Snug-O-Pants Femme for women and Snug-O-Pants Homme for men. To be honest, I don't know which these are supposed to be. You need a theodolite to tell the difference. Next, you have a pair of StinkAways which contain and eliminate smells before they reach the outer world. They are particularly for middle aged men and especially the kind who like real ale and traditional foods and have beards. You know the ones. StinkAways come in grey. Here you have the LuvBucket for the sensual younger woman, though I personally think they should be called sick buckets. They are furry. Grey and furry. They go with the pants in the next image, which are the Man-O-War, the male version of the LuvBucket. Slightly less voluminous than the LuvBucket but equally furry and grey, and equally emetic.'

Victoria sighed.

'Going on, we come to the Gender Benders.'

She sighed again. 'Do I have to?'

'Oh, yes, you are my prisoner.'

'As the name implies, they are unisex underwear. They are a misguided attempt by the makers to show modernity and social relevance. In the name of gender equality, they have created pants that can be worn by both men and women. Sadly, they fail to understand that equality does not consist of everyone cramming their genitals into the same unaccommodating sack. The manufacturers could have done a lot more by setting an example of equality in the workplace for their own employees by giving equal pay and opportunities to the women rather than molesting them with ice cream cones at office parties. The Gender Benders come in grey.

'As do the SecuriSitters, for the older pants-wearer who craves security in those hazardous sitting down moments. And finally, the Kleen-As-U-Go self-cleaning pants. You don't need to wash these so they are ideal for the modern person who is so busy living the modern life, ie, watching TV, that he or she has no time for old-fashioned pursuits such as proper hygiene — or proper eating or proper living. They achieve the self-cleaning property through being impregnated by a cocktail of chemicals so caustic they have been the subject of more than one international environmental conference and more than a few premature deaths. I nearly forgot to mention that they come in grey.'

Victoria sank her head into her hands apparently exhausted.

'There is more,' Kim prompted her.

'They are all manufactured by Hades Undies World, my father's company.'

'Ah, irrefutable proof that you are intimately acquainted with your father's underwear.'

'Oh, please!'

'Now we move on to the next phase of the interrogation.'

With a considerable upgrade of flourish, Kim threw down yet more printed images of undergarments, evidently also from a hard drive inside Hades.

'A change of undergarments!'

'You are not going to make me go through more of these. Please say you won't.'

'Different story this time. Just look. Do you know what these are? These are the alternative lines Hades manufactures. The ones the general public rarely get to hear about, the ones Hades manufactures for various defence departments around the world.

'I bet they all come in shades of grey.'

'So you are aware of these secret weapons!'

'Another lucky guess. What are we talking about here?'

'I'm sure you know.'

Victoria put her hands over her face and then opened her fingers slightly to see the photos.

'Oh, no.'

'I will save you the dilemma of figuring out what we know and what is safe for you to say. The first are the UU-48 Undercover Underpants, the ultimate undercover agents. Woven into the very fabric of these garments are both an omni-directional microphone and a powerful transmitter, with full encryption capabilities and 100GB of flash memory incorporated in the gusset. The vent is also known as the "spy hole" and can accommodate and optional digital camera. These pants turn the wearer into a walking covert eavesdropping device of immense power. The materials are organic and will not show up on security scanners. Imagine just strolling into a meeting with the president of the United States or the CEO of a major arms manufacturer or the head of the CIA and beaming every word back to base. Fantastic!'

'Great, but how do you get the meetings with those people in the first place, and if you are at the meeting you know what is said without having to bug yourself.'

'Shut up!'

'In order to have any spying value, you would have to slip out of the pants during the meeting and hide them in the president's desk in the Oval office or hang them on a lamp shade or slip them over his head without him noticing and then leave them there to transmit his private conversations when you had gone —'

'Shut up!'

'Unless you could knock him out and switch them for his real pants before he recovers.'

'Shut up! You have no respect for your father's work.'

'You spotted that.'

'How about these? Genius! The UU-96 Nautiluses — submersibles for marine operations. They emit bubbles from the seat like scuba gear. Brilliant! The U-PingOffs, armour plated for close-quarter combat. Here are the U-BunkerButts, tactical pants of ultra-advanced carbon fibres that will withstand anything short of a direct hit with a nuclear weapon.' Kim slapped and waved each of the photos in turn. 'These are the Bum Busters, the bouncers; the Geronimo parachuters, the shark repellers, the flame suppressors, the invisible spy pants — just look at the invisible pants! Any military, any secret service that has these, has the world!'

If any of them actually worked, thought Victoria. 'Yah. So you know what these things are, what do you want from me? Lessons on how to put them on?'

'We know what they are. You, Ms Gousset, know how to make them.'

'Uh oh.'

'You will come with us to Pyongyang as a guest of Our Supremely Cuddly Leader and manufacture these inventions of your father's for us.'

'I honestly don't know how to make these things.'

'But you have been involved in your father's business. We know that because of the TV commercials that our spies saw.'

'Yes. I made stuff out of silk and gossamer that made men faint. My father refused to market them. My father made other stuff in my name, things that were better used as tools in opencast mines. Kids used to use that line as fright masks at Halloween. No one dared tell my father the ridicule that his products made in my name were bringing on me. I don't believe he would have cared if he had been told.'

'Well, it is natural that you should be reluctant to come with us because you have never before visited Pyongyang and seen the utopia that it is. Yes, a utopia without equal. We have concrete on every corner! The state-owned department store is *two* stories high and covers as much space as a tennis court. Ah ha! What's more, the store has a can of corned beef on display! Yes! You will like Pyongyang. We eat twigs for breakfast, and we are blessed with the best tasting twigs in the world.

'Now turn off the tape recorder,' Kim commanded his commando-ling, 'and put your fingers in your ears.

'Not you, woman. You are to listen, because it gets better. Oh, yes, much better. In addition to your manufacturing work, the supreme leader himself has chosen you to be. His. Newest. Concubine.'

'What is it that Daddy likes to say at times like these? Ah, yes. Oh, buggery bugger-bags!'

49

Kim left the interrogation room and returned to the main hall. If he had had any worries about his men and the Hashishin coming to well-armed blows while he was out of the room, they were unnecessary. On the contrary, the mood was quite jolly and the main hall was full of chatter. The chatter was not the kind made by conversation. Conversation would be unlikely for two good reasons. First, was the language barrier. Second was the fact that everyone, but everyone in the hall, was stoned beyond reason. The chatter was coming from a lot of — and it took Kim some serious staring to figure out what they were — mechanical, wind up plastic teeth. Kim had not seen anything like them before, but if this was representative of the western culture, the sooner it was consigned to the toilet of history the better.

While he watched, the Hashishin wound up the teeth with a little key on the side, and they went off jumping and chattering on the floor rugs.

His men were also on the floor with their legs in the air, laughing in a most unmilitary way and clearly under the influence of the zany cigarettes the Hashishin were smoking.

Kim's first impulse was to bark at them and demand: Why are you smoking that stuff, aren't you hungry enough already?

His second and more compelling reaction was: Why not? Every minute out of North Korea is a holiday for these men. It'll be back to twigs on Monday.

Kim pulled up abruptly, suddenly self-aware. What am I doing? I'm having thoughts. If Our Scrumptious Leader catches me with thoughts in my head, it'll be re-education camp for me and a diet of sand instead of twigs.

He became aware that Seamus was behind him, staring intently and sucking on a doobie and trying without much competence to do up his trousers.

'Ye all right, there, my man?' Seamus asked, but his eyes were intense and inscrutable.

The world outside the Beloved Homeland is indeed a pernicious place, and the sooner we remove it from the face of the planet, the safer we'll all be, Kim thought and stormed off to check that the rat wheels in the helicopter were properly lubricated.

50

For most of the remainder of the afternoon, Seamus sat alone on the big hospitality rug smoking himself into a cross-eyed state. There was nothing remarkable about this and so no one remarked on it.

It's a shame no one thought anything remarkable about this because something very remarkable indeed was going on: Seamus was thinking deeply about something.

51

Eventually, Kim called his men to the helicopter. It was time for prayers. They strew the rough earth of the fortress top with broken glass and nails, prostrated themselves in the direction of Pyongyang and prayed that their Delectable Leader was having nice time drinking fine brandy, eating scrummy things and laughing to the point of tears at imported American films, while his citizens subsisted on worms and their own nail clippings so he could do so.

They then set about polishing everything in the helicopter while their cook clanged about in the galley pretending to make their imaginary evening meal.

Kim separated himself from his team and stood on the rampart of the towering fortress. He gazed across the desert without seeing anything. Kim had weighty things on his mind.

The Hashishin were not the kind of people he thought them to be. Kim Young-un, the Blushingly Glorious Leader, had apparently sanctioned an alliance with the Hashishin believing them to be a ruthless and dedicated organisation of international jihadists who were hell bent on the overthrow of capitalism and the decadent west. It turned out that the Hashishin were a dedicated disorganisation of international potheads dedicated to the overthrow of the work ethic and the enforcement of nothing in particular. They were people who would use The Fandoobly Leader's superior nuclear technology to force everyone to sit around doing nothing.

This was extremely puzzling.

How could the Most Fantastic Leader in all the World Without Exception have not known about the Hashishin?

Well, he must have known. The Excruciatingly Cool Leader is never wrong. It therefore logically followed that Seamus and the Hashishin were totally wrong about what and who they were; that the Simply Spectacular Leader must know the Hashishin to be vicious, subversives for whom death held no fear, even if the Hashishin thought they were a bunch of layabout potheads.

That made sense.

However, it remained that the Leader, being omniscient, must realise that the Hashishin were wrong about who and what they were. So where did that leave Kim? His infallible leader was asking him, Kim Il-bond, to arm this shower of addled dunderheads even though their values, such as they had any, were completely incompatible with the objectives of The Revolution.

So far so good. What buggered up Kim, here on the roof of Alamut, was that he was the one expected to put a nuke into the hands of these morons. How would that help The Revolution? Clearly, in his infinite wisdom, Kim Young-un had contrived this situation as a personal test for Kim Il-bond.

The sudden understanding caused Kim to swell with pride. Tears came to his eyes. He — lowly, unworthy, Kim Il-bond — had been personally selected for this task and test.

But the understanding did not enable him to see his way through to the successful resolution of the trial. What was he supposed to do? Should he go ahead and provide these dullards with the bomb thus demonstrating unswerving loyalty to his Leader? Or should he do everything to keep the bomb out of their hands? This would show individual initiative in the service of The Revolution but he was not sure that individual initiative was anything the Leader or the Revolution tolerated.

Kim's gaze settled upon the setting sun. He reflected that it was the same sun created and placed in the sky by the grandfather of Kim Young-un, founder of the nation, to guide the revolution with its eternal light, and it was from this sun that Kim now sought illumination.

52

As the sun went down, it washed the Fortress Alamut and the desert in the same rich glow as the morning. Victoria, like Kim Il-bond, on the roof of Alamut, watched from underneath her bucket as the desert and the air dramatically changed colour. As she watched the natural spectacle she came up with some really good ideas for lingerie designs and wondered whether she would ever get home to make them.

53

Seamus called the Hashishin to him.

'Slight change of plan, lads.'

'Have we got a plan?'

A plan? The dismay was palpable.

'Will we have to do anything?' they asked.

'Have you forgotten the plan already? Jesus Christ! The Koreans, why are they here?'

'The Koreans?'

'Yes, the Koreans, the guys on the roof with the whirlybird thing, the people who are one rat short of a flight home.'

'Oh, them. I thought they were here to read the meter,' said the one known as Kenny.

'The meter?'

'Well, they're wearing uniforms and carrying guns, so I naturally thought they were from the electricity company.'

'Aye, I did too,' said Brian.

'Fair dos,' said Seamus, 'but do you not remember us talking about a nuclear weapon?'

'Is that what we were talking about? Was that a real conversation? I thought we were just talking.'

'You may remember,' insisted Seamus, 'that we did a deal with Kim Young-un of North Korea.'

'Nope.' It seemed a unanimous sort of nope.

'Kim Young? Do I know her?' Kenny wondered.

'How young is she?' asked Brian.

'Don't worry, Seamus, we remember you shagged that Kim lass but why has she gone nuclear? Has she found out about your doll?' another Hashishin wanted to know.

'What? No, look, the North Korean mob are here to deliver a nuclear weapon as per a pre-arranged strategic partnership with their country, whose aims are coincident with our own — until we get the nuke and then they can eff off too. But look, the ante has just gone up. Way up.'

'Oh, I'm getting so confused now. Lasses, shags, nuclear things and now floating aunties. Where will it all end?' moaned Kenny.

Seamus tried to get his team back on track. 'You know that lass they have with them? That Victoria? Do you know who she is?'

'Yeah, she's the one with the bucket on her head,' said Brian confidently.

Kenny was not to be left out of knowing things. 'Yeah, I know. Kim called her Victoria or something so I guess she's Victoria.'

'Yes, but do you know who Victoria actually is?'

'I think Victoria might be that lass with the bloke from the lecky upstairs.' This was Brian, experiencing a torrent of knowing things.

'Do you think he's reading her meter? Fnarr, fnarr, fnarr.' Kenny was pleased with his joke but it was a bit difficult for the others.

Seamus was letting his exasperation get to him. 'Look, get another doobie in your face and try to smoke some sense into yourself. This lass is Victoria Gousset, daughter of no less a bloke than Sir Hades Gousset, himself.'

The news dinned some self-awareness into the heads of the Hashishin.

'Sir Hades Gousset?' they asked.

'Yes, the very same.'

'Sir Hades Gousset, the most important man in the world?'

'Absolutely.'

Kenny was a wee bit sceptical. 'How on earth do you

work that out?'

As was Brian. 'Yeah, there's loads of Victorias in the world. How do you know she's precisely Victoria Gousset?'

As were the whole gang. 'To be sure, there's Victoria Secret ...'

'Queen Victoria.'

'There's that Victoria in Australia ...'

'Victoria Station ...'

This could go on forever. 'How do I know it's Victoria Gousset? You know how the bog over there is right next to the little cubbyhole room next to it? And you know how there's a little peeky hole high up for ventilation, which means if you are in the bog you can hear everything going on in the cubbyhole room? Well, I was hunkered down in the poo parlour, helping nature along with a Camberwell Carrot, know what I mean? Well, I heard voices, and it was that Kim bloke interrogating that Victoria lass. And I heard it all. I'm telling you, she's the daughter of Sir Hades, himself.'

'Get away with you. So what would she be doing here? With Kim?'

'Kim's boss, a bloke called, er, Kim, wants her for her knowledge of military technology, which he intends to get from her and put to work in his own army.'

'And what would a pretty slip of a lass know about military technology, now?'

'We're talking about military grade underpants, here, Billy. Combat pants. Spy-wear. The lot. Kim tested her and she knows everything. Once she gets into Kim's military pants, they are going to be unstoppable.'

'Doesn't bear thinking about.'

'And on top of that, the boss Kim wants to shag her.'

'Christ, almighty!'

Kenny had understood Seamus's revelation but was not keeping up with the implications. 'So, we have a celebrity in our humble abode. So what of it Seamus? Are we going to get her autograph?'

'No, lads, we're going to get her, the lass herself. The

nuke and the girl.'

'And what would be the point of that?'

'I thought we was after a nuke. What's the girl got to do with nukes? Does she explode?'

'Better than that, she'll bring the world to its knees before us.'

'Girls. Knees. I thought we had renounced all that for the puff, Seamus.'

'Seamus, now don't be telling us you've got the hots for the lass and that's what this is all about.'

'No, no, no. You're missing the point. It's what she knows we're after. Imagine what her undies know-how can do for us. First off there's the battle pants, military hardware that you can wear; underthings of death. Think what they can do for us.'

'Kill us?'

'No! This technology can help us bring about the spliffate. With these, we can go anywhere, do anything.'

'But we don't want to go anywhere or do anything,' Billy pointed out.

'Isn't that kind of the point of all this? Just chillin' with a pipe?' the Hashishin insisted.

'I know, but until we establish the Spliffate no one's going to leave us alone. It's always going to be, how long are you going to sit there? When are you going to get a job? How about putting a roof on the house? All that shite. We are not going to have the world of peace and calm until straights get off our case.

'Now imagine we all have smart underwear with the capability of doing everything for you. Leaving us with two hands free for the important thing in life.' He mimed rolling papers and tobacco and hash.

Suddenly, Seamus was in danger of engaging the imaginations of the Hashishin.

'Imagine someone is making demands on you. "Get up, do this, do that!" Imagine now you have a pair of underpants that will retaliate. Yes, retaliate for you. We can call them the Undie-manders. Anyone makes demands on you or yours and the Undie-manders go straight for the throat. We don't have to move or anything. A Spliffomatic? You know how you usually put the stash in your pants so the pigs don't find it when they pat you down? How about if the Spliffomatics roll the stuff for you while it's down there? All you have to do is reach into your pants when the police have gone and there's the doobie ready made for you: no need to even move your fingers.

'How about this? Pants that will smoke the stuff for you. Load 'em up, they spark it up. You kick back and the smoke just happens. Great fun for yourself and your intimates, but imagine what they'll do for the Spliffate. We're talking about guerrilla stoning. Put those on and go for a stroll through Wall Street or the City and you'll have the captains of the world's economy dancing in the streets and eating their own money.'

'It'll be like fumigating the world!'

'Now you're getting the idea.'

'Will they make you tea?'

'Now, you're just getting silly. Right. In order to get this done, we've got to get Kim's mob mobile or there'll be no end to this, and no nuke and no girl.'

'I suspect the Koreans will have some opinions about that. And pretty loud ones at that judging by the size of their shooters.'

The Hashishin muttered their agreement and concern. 'Mutter, mutter, mutter,' they said.

'We'll worry about that when we get there,' said Seamus. 'I'm sure they'll just be glad to get the rat and get out of here.'

'Are you sure about that, Seamus? They seem pretty zealous to me.'

'Aw, taking your pants down when you want a poo is zealous for you, Billy.'

'Fair enough.'

'How many rats do we have in the cage, Billy?'

'Five, if you include the dead ones.'

'How many of them are dead?'

'Five.'

'Bugger. Can you not get a live one?'

'Seamus, we're on the top of a mountain in the middle of the bloody desert. How many rats do you think there are round here?'

'Billy, if we switched the rat for a goat, do you think they'd notice?'

'A goat? Are you taking the piss out of my name now, Seamus?'

'No, I'm trying to get a nuke out of them and the girl and then get shot of them. If they don't have something to make that jalopy fly, nothing's going to happen but them eating all our munchies.'

'Well, I could put my mind to it, I suppose.'

'I'd rather you didn't, Billy. We're looking for a result.'

'I'll see what I can do about rats, then.'

'That's what I'm talking about.'

54

'Give me the rat!'

'Give me the nuke!'

Kim's commandos and Seamus's Hashishin were squared off against each other on the roof of Alamut, staring each other out through the sights of their levelled guns. The morning sun was staring down on the men, wondering what on Earth they might be doing and what could possibly be so important to raise passions to such potentially fatally heights, and before breakfast too.

'I'm not leaving without the rat.'

'You most certainly are not. Give me the nuke and I'll give you the rat.'

'How do I know you have a rat?'

'How do I know you have a nuke?'

'Look, I left the nuke somewhere. For safekeeping. Give me the rat and I'll nip out and get the nuke.'

'You must think I'm totally stupid. If I give you the rat, you'll be gone and that will be that. And now you are saying you don't have a nuke at all? If that's the case, you're walking back to Pyongyang.'

'I might have a spare nuke you can use. But I need to know you have a rat.'

'A rat for a nuke. Fair exchange. Give me a moment.'

Seamus went into yet another huddle with his gang. When it broke up the Hashishin wore such looks of gravity and sincerity that Kim became even more alarmed and suspicious. Kim observed that the one known as Billy was absent. This was odd because he was usually glued to Seamus's side.

'OK, Kim, I'm back.'

'Do you have a rat?'

'Do I have a rat? Do I have a rat, he's asking. What I've got is better than a rat. Jeez, I must be mad offering you this for one nuke. I should now be asking for a whole shed-full of hydrogen bombs for this and the shed too. But what's a gesture of goodwill if it's not a gesture of goodwill, if you know what I mean?'

'I don't know what you mean. No, rat, no nuke.'

'As I say, you'll love this. When I tell you what I'm offering, you'll wonder why you ever thought you wanted a scabby old rat. What I'm offering is a whole ... goat. Now, you can't say better than that? A whole goat for one measly nuke. You're impressed now, I can tell.'

Kim lowered his weapon in exasperation.

'A goat? What good is a goat to me other than as a sandwich?'

'What good is a goat to you? The ingratitude of you! Have you never heard the expression, don't look a gift goat in the mouth? A goat is much, much bigger than a rat and is therefore worth, I dunno, dozens of rats. I think I will ask for that shed full of hydrogen bombs, after all.'

'This helicopter runs on rat power. How will I get a goat in the rat wheel?'

'Don't you military types like to use your initiative? Fold it up, or something.'

'Just give me a rat and we'll all be on our way.'

'Will you take a chicken?'

Kim was suddenly red and spitty. 'No, I want a rat. What does R, A, T spell? It spells fucking rat. And what's a synonym of fucking rat? Fucking nuke, that's what. If a fucking rat is equivalent to a fucking nuke, then it follows that no fucking rat means no fucking nuke. How fucking difficult can it be?'

Billy appeared at Seamus's side and whispered in his

ear: 'Seamus, I think we're sorted in the rat department. But make it snappy, whatever you're doing, it's more of a rat workaround than a rat fix, if you see what I mean.'

'Brilliant!' Seamus whispered at Billy. 'I don't think he was totally getting the goat and chicken thing.' Back to Kim, whose gun was back up and whose finger was twitching on the trigger. 'OK. A rat it is, but I think you're a mug for turning down the goat and the chicken. Let's see the nuke then. I'll show you the rat when I see the big firework. I'll show you mine if you show me yours. To the Hashishin, 'Give me a fucking toke, I think we're nearly there.'

Momentarily, Kim looked uncertain then turned and leaped into the helicopter. There was a lot of loud banging and thumping and lots of words in Korean that didn't really need any translation. After a particularly loud clatter, he emerged carefully cradling a silver, cylindrical object.

'Careful. It has a built in trembler, which means that any sudden movement could make it go off. It's very sensitive.'

Seamus was sceptical. 'It looks like a large thermos to me.'

'Of course it looks like a thermos. Have you ever seen a thermonuclear device that didn't look like a thermos?' retorted Kim who was speaking like someone who didn't want to shout in case it caused the nuclear bomb they were carrying to go off.

Seamus had never seen a thermonuclear device and therefore found it logically impossible to respond to Kim's question with anything other than no.

'No. I suppose not.'

'What's it supposed to look like? A teapot? An aspidistra?' asked Kim, pressing home his point.

'An aspidistra would be nice,' said Seamus, cocking his head to one side to better imagine the bomb as a pot plant.

'Now where are the rodents?'

Billy stepped forward with the cage, in which five rats were frantically animated and hopping and bouncing about. One was bouncing on its back with its legs in the air.

'There you are.'

It was Kim's turn to be sceptical. It seemed to him that Seamus was trying to suppress a look of surprise on his own face. 'What are the rats doing? Are they all right?'

'Oh, Jesus, yes. They're just totally psyched about the trip. Great travellers, rats,' Billy assured him.

'That one's sort of jiggling on its back. What's with that?'

'Erm, he's break dancing. Street rat, isn't it. Not like your sewer rat. Much more sophisticated. Will wear his hat backwards if he can get his paws on one.'

'Look, I'm going to need to check those rats,' declared Kim.

'And I'm going to need to check that nuke, now you come to mention it.' Seamus seemed to have recovered from his surprise.

'Oh, damn, is that the time?' asked Kim, theatrically looking at his watch. 'We need to be getting back. Let's just get on with the exchange.'

Billy made to approach Kim with the cage of rats, but Seamus stepped in his way.

'Ah, now there's one more thing. I want the girl. So that's five rats from me, and one nuclear weapon and one girl from you. Thank you very much.'

'You want the girl? You're changing the deal at the last minute?'

'No one's changing the deal. This was the deal all along. I am just now apprising you of the full scope of the arrangement. And now you are fully apprised, you can hand over the girl and the bomb and we can be on our various ways.' Seamus seemed very confident of the state of affairs.

'So you think you are going to take the girl and the bomb and that will be that.'

'Pretty much. Unless you want a toke. Do you want a toke? Give us a puff, lads, this is going on longer than I thought.'

'Well, you're not getting the girl and the nuke. What do

you think of that? Our agreement was for one thermonuclear device in exchange for one living rat. And that's what's going to happen. The girl belongs to Our Big Fluffy Huggable Leader and not to you. She's not up for negotiation.'

Victoria, huddled glumly in the back of the helicopter, heard this and felt unclean. 'No, I bloody don't belong to anyone,' she said aloud, not that anyone was listening to her.

'Look, man, that's not just one rat, that's five rats. How can you say no to bunging in the totty?'

'I only asked for one rat. And now you're pushing five of the stinking animals on me.'

Billy barged in. 'They're not stinking. I washed them all in formaldehyde myself. Carbolic, I mean.'

'OK, OK. I'll throw in the goat but I'm beginning to feel robbed,' said Seamus.

'Just give me a rat!'

'A goat, five rats and a chicken.'

The rats in question were suddenly looking a lot less animated than they had been just a minute ago. Their collective jitterbugging had slowed to just bugging.

'Ah, said Billy, let me just take them out back and wind them up, I mean perk them up a bit out of the sun.'

'I've got a better idea,' snarled Kim. 'Why don't I just come down there and take them for myself?'

'Nah, you wouldn't do that. You've got every Hashishin in the world pointing guns at you. I think you'd better take this deal and be off while the going's good.'

'Every Hashishin in the world? Guns? Don't make me laugh. You're so stoned I'm amazed your feet can find the ground. On the other hand, you, my little friend, are staring death in the face, death in the shape of North Korea's especially special forces. You don't get more trained in the dark art of dishing out death and destruction than these heroic sons of the glorious motherland. If you want to retain only the standard number of orifices in your body, you had better just put the rats down where I can see them and walk away now.'

'Rats? Goats? Chickens? Thermos flasks? Is that all I'm worth to you people?' Victoria was on her feet in the door of the helicopter. She was thoroughly fed up of being stowed in the back of the chopper listening to this inane drivel from her captors.

'It's not a thermos, it's a thermonuclear device,' said Kim and Seamus together.

'I don't care what it is. I'm not something that can be bargained over like a sack of potatoes. I'm a free woman, not a chattel.'

Kim and Seamus glanced at each other. 'Ooh! Hark at her!'

'Bad hair day, is it?'

'I thought all women were chattel-boxes,' spluttered Billy.

'And look at you. A bunch of macho dickheads, bigging yourselves up in front of each other with oh-so-important plans and schemes and your big-gun toys. You're dribbling morons, the lot of you.'

The Hashishin collectively could no longer contain themselves.

'Oh, is it that time of the month already?'

Snort!

'I get it, it's a rag week lark.'

Sniggers.

'Who said that? Victoria grabbed the first thing that came to hand which happened to be a flare gun clipped to the inside wall of the helicopter — only to be used in the case of emergencies — and flung it at whichever Hashishin she thought had spoken last. Not that she cared who had spoken last. They and Seamus and Kim and Kim's crew were all the same to her: a bunch of kidnapping male wankers.

It was a beautiful and powerful throw and the flare gun landed right between the eyes of the guy who had indeed launched the last facile excuse for a joke. The flare gun went off shooting a fizzing, whizzing ball of flame into the ranks of the Koreans where it burst, gushing red smoke. At the same time the Hashishin's gun went off, spraying bullets into the air. The commandos reacted in the way that commandos do, by diving for cover and returning fire. This brought another fusillade from the Hashishin, which led to a predictable round of fire on fire.

Bullets pinged and whined around the top of the ancient fortress. The Koreans, wreathed in red smoke had scant idea where they were shooting. The Hashishin wreathed in pot smoke had less idea.

Kim and Seamus moved fast.

Kim tossed away the nuclear weapon and dived for the rats. Seamus dived for the bomb, which he caught in mid air on some long-dormant reflex of catching tossed cookies.

'Billy, to you!' The same reflex sent the bomb to Billy in a spinning, torpedo of a back pass. In one movement Seamus hurled himself into the helicopter, threw Victoria over his shoulder, leapt out the far door of the chopper and legged it into the nearest stairwell, back into the interior of the fortress.

Kim handed off the cage of rats to his own number two and gave chase.

55

Seamus hurtled through the tunnels of Alamut with Victoria helplessly thrown across his shoulders. The fortress was ancient and its interior, burrowed in the living rock of the mountain was without light — light, being, presumably, a distraction to the monastically inclined inhabitants all those hundreds of years ago.

Victoria beat on Seamus's back and legs and tried kicking his face or chest, but made no impression on him. She flung out her legs and arms in the hope of grabbing onto something or gaining purchase on the walls but all she did was hurt herself on unseen objects. Bats took fright at their passing and flapped around them.

'Calm down, be still,' she told herself. 'Think!'

And in that calm moment she felt the history, the soul of Alamut. As much as it was a fortress, it was also a place of learning and meditation, a place of devotion and wisdom. And yet it was also a place of training for a special kind of soldier, the Nizari equivalent of the ninja, the original assassins whose weapons were darkness and cunning.

The story went that 800 years before, when the fortress Alamut, Hassan-i-Sabbah and the original Hashishin were at the peak of their power and influence, the Seljuk sultan Sanjar tried to crush the Naziris. He rode his army at Alamut. Surely even this fortress would crumble before the onslaught of his army. The army made camp. Sanjar woke one morning with a dagger planted in the ground by his head. It was a gentle message from the Hashishin. If they could get him in his tent while he was asleep, they could get him anywhere ... and on this occasion they had let him live.

Sanjar called off his war against the Naziri.

Something of the spirit of Alamut was now entering Victoria: the wisdom of the ages; the guile of the original Hashishin.

Suddenly, she knew what she had to do.

It wasn't easy navigating in Seamus's Pashtun outfit, but she persevered and managed to insert both hands inside his baggy trousers. She took a firm grip on his underpants and yanked upwards. Seamus stiffened, screamed and pitched headlong to the ground.

Victoria was thrown forward by the impetus, but dark was now her friend. She found her feet and leapt on Seamus's prone form. She took hold again on the waistband of his pants, which was now somewhere around his chest, and pulled again with all her might. Again, Seamus screamed, and then screamed some more. Moments later he fell silent, then he went limp, completely passed out.

Victoria knew she had only seconds to act and swiftly debagged the unconscious man. She had never actually debagged and unconscious man before — and an insufficient number of conscious ones, in her opinion — but circumstances were making her resourceful. Clutching his pants, she stepped back into a recess — more sensed than seen — in the tunnel wall just as Kim came upon them.

Discovering the prone form on the floor, Kim paused to investigate, In that moment Victoria stepped out behind him and jammed Seamus's pants over his head. She twisted them tight and pulled with all her might. Kim struggled. He was a very strong man and Victoria knew she had no way of overpowering him before the underpants did, so using his own body weight she stepped aside and made sure that as Kim lurched his head connected with the wall. Roaring inside the foul head wrap, he retaliated, swinging his whole body, attempting to use his own larger bulk against Victoria. She again sidestepped and guided his head into the other wall, while keeping a firm hold on the pants on his head. That was all Kim could deal with. He sagged to the floor and was still, as unconscious as Seamus.

There, the small, lonely woman had overpowered two armed men using only her courage and her specialist knowledge of underwear.

After handling the Hashishin's pants, Victoria felt she needed a shower but there was no time for niceties. Following the instincts the spirit of Alamut had given her, she plunged on in the dark until she found what she was looking for: an aperture in the fortress wall. Whether it was a window or a door was hard to tell; it was a hole and it was a way out and she took it.

Victoria found herself on the lower slopes of the hill that housed Alamut. Before her, a wide plane covered in sand and rocks and tufty bits of scrub and the odd stray goat; behind her, captivity and a lot of very silly men with guns. There was a volley of shots from the roof, where, presumably, the silly men were still fighting over the thermos and the rats.

Well, they bloody well weren't fighting over her any longer.

She set off into the desert with nothing to guide her but hope.

56

We are on crowded planet Earth, Victoria reasoned. How far can you go before bumping into some bit of humanity?

Actually in some parts of the planet you can walk until you die without finding an iota of civilisation, but we are not going to put that thought in Victoria's head at this moment.

A related thought is that you can travel great distances through massive, thriving cities and their conurbations without finding an iota of civilisation, either, but now we are getting complicated.

Victoria's supposition about the proximity of humanity was confirmed after an hour when she happened on a road of sorts. It was half submerged by drifting dust but it did have a black top. Somebody at some point had thought to go to the bother of building it here and so that somebody must have had the expectation that somebody else would use it. She followed the road with more hope.

Another hour went by.

While the road spoke of civilisation, the absence of anything on it did not. It was entirely possible, of course, that the somebody who had built the road had failed to tell the somebody else they expected to travel it that the road was actually available for use. That somebody else might at that moment be actually somewhere, going nowhere, wishing there was a road to take them somewhere else without realising that just such a road had been built especially for them for that very purpose. If that were the case, the someone who had built the road must be a friend of Seamus or Kim. But that is all speculation and has no place here.

Forensic examination of the blacktop revealed that the dust on it was looking very undisturbed. No tyre tracks. No footprints. No empty drinks cans or crisp wrappers to suggest travellers had ever been that way.

There was a dumped fridge, but they are everywhere. They fall from the sky.

The afternoon heat was drying Victoria out. She came across a rough, earth-walled thing that might have been a goatherd's shelter. It was indeed full of goat poo. It might have been a goat shelter, or a goat lavatory. It might be a bus stop, it might be the main parliament building for whatever country she was in, she didn't know. It did keep her out of the sun for the worst of the afternoon.

Discounting the poo, there were still no signs of life.

When the shadows lengthened she set off again. She was thirsty, tired, hungry, dirty and in serious need of a change of underwear.

The afternoon turned into dusk, which changed into night and Victoria plodded along for lack of anything else to do.

She found herself searching the pockets of her grey baggies for something to eat, something she may have absent-mindedly stashed earlier and forgotten about. Perhaps a sweet. A stick of dried goat meat. A handful of corn flakes. A bottle of water. An enormous stick of French bread stuffed with cold meats, cheeses, salad and olives that she had forgotten about. There was nothing.

A few minutes later she searched her two pockets again in case she had missed anything before. She still had not.

Soon after that she searched again in case something had materialised there at random since the last search. Nothing had.

She quickly went back looking for lint to eat. There was plenty of that.

How long can a person go without food, she wondered. She calculated the time that had passed since breakfast. About that long, she concluded.

She also noticed that just a week before she would not have been able to do that calculation, nor would she have known what the word meant. How long could one survive without a drink? Well, she'd had wine and cocktails at Schloss Himmel and although she could do with one now, she didn't feel about to keel over if she didn't. She was, however, terribly thirsty for water of all things. Was that normal?

The black of the night was dense. Where blackness had been her friend in the fortress, it most certainly was not here. The night threatened. The night whispered at her of how lost and alone and far away from home she was and how vulnerable. The blackness mocked her.

Looking up, she had a fantastic view of the stars. Unimpeded by cloud or city light or pollution, they shone with the full glory of the Milky Way. The sight did not delight her. The infinity and coldness of space just another reminder her of how small and insignificant and lost she was at that moment.

She avoided looking up, and cupped her hands round her eyes to keep the vastness of space out of them.

Had she marvelled a bit more at infinity, she would have noticed that one of the stars was moving in a most un-star-like manner. She would have seen it getting closer, drifting out of the cosmos and down toward the desert. She would have noticed that it appeared to be spinning. She would have found it quite remarkable that not only was it heading for the desert, it appeared to be heading directly for her.

It wasn't until the thing — for that is most definitely what it was, a thing — was hovering over her dousing her in its glow that she realised it was there.

'Oh,' said Victoria. 'That's not the kind of civilisation I was hoping to encounter.'

Twin arms of light focused on her. It was an odd sort of light as it seemed to have some sort of substance, and that substance enveloped her — which wasn't at all unpleasant — and lifted her off the ground drawing her up toward the bright thing — which *was* decidedly unpleasant.

An aperture opened. She was drawn inside.

'Oh, buggery bugger-bags,' said Victoria. 'I've been kidnapped again. By aliens.'

57

The opulent and sprawling Gousset family home, in its own land equivalent to the size of a county, might ordinarily be called a Georgian pile. Having been for several days on the end of Persephone's frustration it is now just a pile.

'It's your fault.'

'No, it's your fault.'

'If you hadn't kidnapped her from Villa Parque she'd be here with us now.'

'If I hadn't kidnapped her from Villa Parque, she'd still be there holding this family to ransom. At least she knew where she was. And on the same boot, if you hadn't kidnapped her from me, she wouldn't have been kidnapped by Maul and Flay.'

'Oh, yeah? And how do you know Maul and Flay wouldn't have kidnapped her from you? What made you think you could trust them?'

'They wouldn't dare kidnap anyone from me, that's why. They would bloody well know what I would do to them if they crossed me.'

'Well, they did bloody well kidnap from you! They stole your daughter!'

'They kidnapped her from you not me. They didn't double cross me, they double crossed you!'

'If you hadn't used Maul and Flay to kidnap Victoria I

wouldn't have known you trusted them and I wouldn't have trusted them, so don't try to put the blame on me!'

Persephone absentmindedly ripped the mantelpiece from above the fire and hurled it at Hades' head.

'And if you hadn't tried to rescue her at Disneyland, I would have got her back.'

'Oh, that's rich! After seeing that Maul and Flay were absolutely not to be trusted you trusted them to return Victoria after you had given them all that cash. At least I tried to rescue her instead of just laying down whatever they wanted with a crap-eating grin and an invitation to walk all over us with spiky shoes.'

'It was your bloody incompetent rescue attempt that got her kidnapped by bloody Mickey Mouse in a pair of leopard print trunks.'

'That was Timmy, for God's sake!'

'Even better, you had her kidnapped by a dead man with Mickey Mouse's head and leopard print trunks. How did you do that? Imagine what the neighbours will say when they come round for Pimm's. "And where's Victoria this fine day? Joining us for Pimm's is she?" "Well, no actually, her father screwed up on the Dumbo ride and got her abducted by a deceased moron in fancy dress." "Oh, that's nice." "More Pimm's vicar?"'

A suit of armour came in low and screaming at him. He sidestepped it only to see its mace following at equal velocity. He had to roll to avoid that.

He emerged from the dust and rubble to see Persephone, all akimbo standing over him.

'You know you have to get her back. I miss her terribly and I'm worried sick.'

Hades may have been a bag of middle-aged testosteronal obstinacy, but he wasn't completely mad. He took his wife in his arms and told her, 'We'll get her back. I've put all the resources of Pants Corp on the case. I've also been on to every world leader and told each of them what will happen to their economies if they don't pitch in help track Victoria down. Timmy doesn't stand a chance of getting away with this.'

'But they could be anywhere in the world. After Disneyland we haven't a clue where they went. How on earth could anyone pick up a trail that cold?'

'On earth, perhaps we couldn't. Off earth is a different matter,' said a third voice, apparently from nowhere.

'Hilda!'

Hades' personal assistant Hilda Titanium stepped carefully through a gap on the wall.

'I'm terribly sorry to intrude without knocking. There didn't seem to be anything to knock on.'

'What are you talking about with this "off Earth" stuff?' Hades demanded.

'We believe we have a lead on Victoria.'

'By Jove, that's fantastic!'

'Where is she? Is she OK?'

'I stress, a lead. At least we think we know where Timothy is, and if we know where Timothy is, that's a lead on Victoria.'

'Go on, Hilda. Tell us everything.'

'Well, your calling around got the planet mobilised, Sir Hades. America got its drones up and its spy birds on the job. Russia got its spooks on the ground. China — well, they just spread the word through the diaspora and had eyes and ears in every corner of every Chinese restaurant in the world in minutes. MI6 made tea for all involved. Everyone, but everyone, pitched in.'

'So was it the drones or the satellites or the spies or the Chinese restaurateurs that found her?'

'None of the above.'

'Oh.'

'We also had help from science.'

'From science?'

'Yes, from science. Science in space.' Hilda clicked a video to play on her tablet and held it up for Hades and Persephone to see. It was the video of the debacle in Disneyland from Persephone's hat. Hades winced.

Smoke billowed, people ran screaming, the Dumbos swooped in low and piled up, the Mickey cartwheeled in and finally ... there was no Victoria.

'Now, observe closely,' Hilda instructed. She reversed the footage and froze the frame on Timmy. 'Look closely. Do you notice anything?'

'He looks like an idiot, but we don't need science to figure that out for us.'

'Yes, but look again.'

'Nope. You've lost me, I afraid. What are we looking for?'

'Timothy's leopard print trunks!' announced Hilda triumphantly but unhelpfully.

'What of them?'

'Ringing no bells?'

'I might have seen those trunks on a big cat while on safari.' Hades shrugged. 'Did I shoot it?'

'The trunks are made by Hades, which is convenient. We were able to identify the exact dyes and colours used in their manufacture and calculate the exact spectral wavelengths of each and every colour shade and hue from the original patterns.

'We were then able to collate that data to get an exact spectral profile of the design — which, thanks to Victoria's creativity in designing, is unique. We then distributed the profile to every space-based spectrometer. There are a few of those. They scan the stars. The light signature of anything floating around up there tells the boffins lots and lots about its chemical composition, spin, size, mass, what the inhabitants had for tea, whatever, and because the stars they are studying are so far away these spectrometers have to be incredibly sensitive.'

'Sensitive enough,' broke in Persephone, catching the drift, 'to spot a pair of distinctively patterned trunks at a distance of several hundred kilometres.'

'Exactly, so we got the boffins to turn their space-based spectrometers around and point them down here. And bingo's your uncle. In less than a day we got a result.'

'So where is Victoria? We must get going at once.'

'Ah! As I said, we have located the trunks, and probably Timothy. I cannot guarantee what we'll find when we get there.'

'But where's there?'

'Switzerland. The Alps. A mountain named Teufel which happens to be host to a certain castle named Schloss Himmel, which has historical ties to Timothy's family, who were forced to flee the nation several generations ago for putting up the same castle without planning permission.'

'Are they still there? Can we catch them?'

Hilda swished to another screen on her tablet. 'The trunks have not moved since we spotted them. But now we have a fix on them, they won't get away. I have helicopters being prepared on the pad here at your pad, and special forces from umpteen different Nato nations and Switzerland itself are getting in position to swoop. What say we join them?'

'What do you mean the trunks are made by Hades? Not possible. Wouldn't be seen dead flogging tat like that. Nothing sensible about them. Daft pants, they are. Frippery. You don't gird your loins in frippery, you know.'

'Victoria does.'

'Harrumph! And harrumph again, I say! That's my daughter you're talking about.'

'I'm afraid it's true,' said Persephone softly. 'You know those very non-sensible underthings she designed?'

'No daughter of mine wears leopard print trunks.'

'Not leopard print trunks. She designed those for men at the same time she was designing creations of her own. Well, in addition to the ones you rejected and forbade her from manufacturing, she's been continuing to design these creations, and make prototypes.'

'No. It couldn't be.'

'More than that, she has been wearing them.'

'Good Lord! Impossible!'

'On a day-to-day basis.'

'I can't listen.'

'She eschewed wearing your officially designated Hades sensibles a number of years ago.'

'Tell me it isn't so! My daughter? Wearing ... wearing those things? No daughter of mine ever would!'

'No one ever wanted to tell you, Hades, but it's been kind of an open secret.'

'My daughter's underpants are an open secret?'

'Well, not in those words, and by everyone we only mean those who do her laundry and work in her studio. Not everyone on the planet. Well, when I say not everyone on the planet, I mean other than the readers of the magazine she publishes called *Victoria Gousset Personally Models Her Own Daring Creations*, but it only has a circulation of seven billion or so, so that's not quite everyone on the planet.

'Magazine? Modelling? Studio?'

'Yes, the business you set up for her within the Hades group but whose products you won't permit on the market.'

'But, but — that wasn't supposed to actually make anything. That was just a toy thing for her. What is she doing designing these ... frilly frills of pink nothing? And then *wearing* them?'

'She's just being herself, Hades.'

'Has she learned nothing from me? Did I not bring her up to appreciate sensible underthings? Did I not provide her with everything she needed whenever she needed it?'

'She learned plenty from you, Hades. She learned she didn't like being swaddled in scratchy flannel. She learned she didn't appreciate being treated like a possession. She learned she was an individual with feelings. She learned she needed to grow and discover her own potential.'

'No!'

'I'm sorry Hades. But that's the way it is. And truth be told, that's probably why she went off and kidnapped herself. It was probably her way of demanding to be taken seriously.'

'But of course I take her seriously. I always have. I have never taken anyone so seriously. I take her more seriously than my own life.'

'Well, I don't want to sound combative, Hades, dear, but you take what you think her life ought to be more seriously than you take your own life. Perhaps you could consider taking what she considers her own life a bit more seriously.'

'Pah and tosh!' thundered Hades. 'Oh, buggery bugger-bags!' and he stormed out through one of the holes in the wall, the tremors of his passing causing more lumps of masonry to fall.

'Well that went well.'

'I'm so terribly sorry, Persephone. I didn't intend to create a shit storm.'

'Oh, it's Hades and I who have created the shit storm. We're the ones who are sorry. But didn't I do well? I haven't demolished anything or thrown anything for at least five minutes.'

Hilda stopped and looked round at the moonscape of rubble that used to be a perfectly good mock-Georgian mansion of extravagant proportions. 'I'm not sure there was anything left to knock down.'

'Oh, I haven't uprooted the basement yet. Now, we'd better catch up with Hades. He'll be waiting for us so we can get to Switzerland together.'

'But I thought he just stormed off in a blazing mood.'

'Never mind that. It's just his way of saying he was wrong. Let's get on.'

58

Hades One, a very fast private jet zoomed the Goussets, Hilda Titanium and their entourage to Geneva, where they switched to an improbably large helicopter, which in turn took to the skies to rendezvous with a huge fleet of whirlybirds carrying rescue personnel from every friendly nation on the planet. There were special forces, mountain rescue, coast guard, air-sea rescue, animal rescue, the Automobile Association, and, courtesy of the Swiss government, a large, shaggy St. Bernard with a barrel of brandy slung about its neck.

NASA continued to confirm the GPS coordinates of Timmy's trunks. Ominously, they hadn't moved since they had been spotted.

The massive fleet of helicopters thundered through the idyllic valleys of the Alps. The ground below shook, instantly churning milk to butter, to the delight of those farmers whose milk was in the churns, and to the chagrin of those whose milk was still in the cows.

The airborne armada rose into the snowy mountain passes of the Alps and finally, the brick and mortar fantasy that was Schloss Himmel came into view, perched atop its mountain like a very regal crown.

The fleet buzzed the towers of Schloss Himmel, binoculars, infrared and thermal cameras, electromagnetometers and phone cameras trained on the mountain; the high tech stuff searching for signs of life, and the phone cameras searching on the off chance they caught anything that could go on YouTube.

The pilot of the Gousset's helicopter was humming Wagner's *Flight of the Valkyries*.

'We have a clear fix on a spot on one of the lower slopes of the mountain, Sir Hades,' announced the operation commander over a video link direct to a screen in front of Hades' Captain Kirk chair on the flight deck of the helicopter.

'Take, us in, please.'

'Shouldn't we secure the area first?'

'This is Timmy we are talking about: a steroid-addled slab of meat with an appalling taste in clothes. We ourselves are in no danger though our aesthetic sensibilities might be.'

The helicopter pilot located a clearing and set down in a self-made snowstorm. The flakes of which were still settling as Hilda, still following directions from the Hubble on her tablet, led Hades and Persephone to where Timmy ought to be.

The spot turned out to be a large snowdrift from which two bare, blue legs protruded.

Without waiting for any help to arrive, the three of them dug Timmy out with their own hands and then continued to search fruitlessly through the drift for Victoria.

Hilda had the presence of mind to stand back and call medical help for Timmy, and set in motion a full search and forensic sweep of the area.

Very soon the mountainside was smothered with trained rescue experts wading through the snow shouting expertly and forensically, 'Yoo hoo! Victoria! Where are you?'

59

A search of the Schloss Himmel yielded only piles of dead animals, lichen, suspicious-wee smelling wet patches of melted snow, and the bones of planning permission enforcers trapped in the castle two hundred years previously.

Hades had taken over the grand hall as a de facto base for the search. His teams installed satellite dishes, computers, and coffee machines. They strode about meaningfully showing each other important data on the screens of their tablets — or showing each other funny cat videos on YouTube.

'It's as if Victoria disappeared from the face of the planet,' boomed Hades. 'Can anyone tell me what has happened here? What does that Timmy have to say for himself?'

A conveniently adjacent doctor was at least able to fill him on the latter question.

'We have been thawing Mr Adonis. It seems he has been subject to a couple of boos lately. The first, at least a week ago just missed him, leaving incidental tissue trauma. The second was more serious and much more recent and was a direct hit. Mr Adonis survived because the boo miraculously careened off his steroids. If it weren't for the sheer quantity of gym candy stacked in there he'd be a goner. He was also fortunate that he ended up in the snow, which reduced his body temperature and sent him into suspended animation, which kept him nice and fresh, if a tad frost bitten, until we got to him. We have been thawing him slowly and carefully so that he doesn't get chewy.'

'But what does he tell us about Victoria?'

'That she didn't like the yellow snow. We're still trying to decode that.'

'But what else did he say? Surely he knows something about Victoria and her whereabouts.'

'Likely he does, but he's in no state to tell us. It will be a while before he can speak coherently, if indeed he will ever be able to with all those arnolds in him.'

'Curses! Our best lead adrift in his own drool. Where does that leave us? Now, where is Hilda? When things seem blackest she generally manages to pull some good news out of the hat. Ah! Here she is now. How now, saint Hilda! What glad tidings?'

'Rat poo.'

'Damn, I was so hoping you would have something positive to tell me.'

'Oh, but I do. Rat poo!'

'So you keep saying.'

'Bear with me. We found quite a pile of rat poo on the roof. What does that tell you?'

'Rats. That's what it tells me. Brown furry things with an awful hygiene problem and a personality to match. This is a very old castle, I'm sure the place is running with them.'

'Check that thought, Sir Hades. It's an old castle for sure, but where is it?'

'Switzerland. Don't they have rats in Switzerland, or did the wooden cuckoos peck 'em all to death?'

'Oh, Sir Hades. It's the trauma of losing Victoria, it has to be, because you are missing the bare-tailed obvious.'

'Oh. I see what you mean. We're perched on top of near-sheer, rocky, snow-covered mountain. What would rats be doing on the roof or any other part of the place? You mean ... rats made off with Victoria? Threw her off the roof?'

'No, but there's more. A few nights ago, Nato picked up the radar signature of a North Korean special forces helicopter in this very neighbourhood. They didn't do anything because it was, well, North Korean. It was probably out scavenging for food for the starving masses or buying brandy and crisps from the Budget Mart for President Kim Young-un — or so Nato assumed.'

'But didn't the North Koreans eat all their rats in one or other of their famines?'

'Some were saved for the special forces helicopters, to keep the rotors going by running in dynamo wheels.'

'By big-jobby Jove — you mean the North Koreans have got Victoria?'

'Forensics have suggested that Timmy's boo was delivered with a Pyongyang accent. I think we know who the naughty boys are.'

'Brilliant! But, you don't suppose they'll eat her, do you? Not a moment to lose. Let's invade North Korea.'

'If I may, Sir Hades, there's one more thing you need to know. The helicopter doesn't appear to have reached North Korea. It disappeared off Nato's radars when it left Turkish air space and went into the mountains of north Iran. It hasn't been seen since.'

'Iran, eh? A closed theocracy, enemy of the west, armed to the teeth and beyond. What is it I like to say on these occasions? Ah, yes. Oh, buggery bugger-bags!'

60

Conveniently somebody's army corps of engineers placed an impressive conference table in the middle of the castle hall. Inlaid on it's top was the Hades Undies World corporate logo, surrounded by the flags of the UN, Nato and all the nations and organisations participating in the search for Victoria.

Hades and Hilda and their crew planted themselves around the table and assumed dejected postures.

The magnate summed up the mood. 'Bloody North Korea. Bloody Iran. Where do we go from here?

'OK. Point everything we have at Iran. The country is only 1,648,195 square kilometres and the 18th largest in the world, so finding a mere slip of a girl will be a doddle,' said Hades heavily. 'Can we try that spectrometer thing again? It worked spiffingly with Timmy.'

'Sorry Hades, we can't get a fix on the colour of those baggies she was wearing in the Disneyland video. The colour was so drab the instruments of Hubble's sensitivity won't respond to it.'

'Make way,' chimed Persephone, marching into the hall with her own retinue. 'We're here to get Victoria back.'

Hades rolled his eyes but sat up attentively. 'And how are we going to do that, sweetness? I think we have most of the world's finest intelligence-gathering brains on the job with all the electronic hardware that the planet can muster and we haven't yet figured out how to trace her.'

'You're thinking in straight lines, Hades. I've told you it gets you nowhere. What we really need to get Victoria back is a whopping and scrummy tea with lots of sticky buns. The more sticky buns the better.'

'Persephone ...' began Hades but his wife cut him off with some loud claps of the hands. 'Come on, get those napkins tucked into your collars. You are going to scoff for Victoria whether you like it or not.'

'Persephone ...' began Hades but a loud clapping look in her eyes cut him off.

A procession of waiting staff in crisp, white jackets and crisp, sharp expressions and crisp, immaculate manners entered the hall bringing with them, aloft on silver trays, a heavenly feast of teatime goodies. Tea, coffee, jam, scones, butter, cream, more tea, cakes, and, especially, a huge quantity of sticky buns. And not just any old sticky buns, but all sorts of sticky buns from a selection of Europe's foremost makers of buns that were sticky. A collection of stickier, bunnier buns had never been collected in one place in the history of human doings with sticky buns. It was a world fair of stickiness and bunniness.

'Now, I want you all to come and sit at this end of the table in a big happy smiley crowd. You may not feel like smiling or eating sticky buns, but if you want Victoria back on one piece, that's exactly what you'll do.'

Exchanging glances but not daring to comment, Hades and Hilda and their various staff and the various chiefs of staff of the world's armed forces and their staff moved up to Persephone's end of the conference table.

'Now I want to see everyone with those napkins tucked in the neck and generally tucking in to tea. Like this, Hades, a bun in each hand and one in the mouth. There's a good boy.

'Can I have my computer in front of me, now?'

Another member of staff brought her laptop on yet another silver platter. It was already booted up and running.

'Please put it a bit further back, more towards the

middle of the table. I want the camera to catch as many of the buns as possible, as well as all of us scoffing them ... That's good.'

'Mwuph mwumm mwumumm?' asked Hades, who was discovering the challenges of articulating round a sticky bun.

'Skype, dear. Basically, I'm using a bit of simple psychology to find out where our daughter is.'

'Mwimph mwim mwum?'

'Well, think about it. Who last had Victoria?'

'Muwmum mim.'

'Yes, the North Koreans. And what do we know about the North Koreans?'

'Mmimum ummum.'

'Exactly. They're always hungry. So how do we get information out of them?'

'Immi ums.'

'Now we're on the same page. OK everyone, get stuck in and follow my lead.' She clicked the call button in Skype, and somewhere thousands of kilometres away, there was an imitation telephone warble on another computer.

'Hello?' The image of Kim Young-un cobbled itself together out of big lumpy brick-like pixels.

'President Kim! Or should I call you Dearest, Darlingest, Gorgeousest Leader? How are you this day?' Persephone took an enormous bite out of an especially sticky bun, perhaps the stickiest on the table. The Korean president's eyes widened and he slapped his lips with his tongue.

'Mrs Gousset. How nice to speak to you again — and so soon.'

Getting the idea, Hades, Hilda, Catshit and the rest grabbed handfuls of the buns and crammed them in their mouths, noisily washing them down with big slurps of tea.

'But how are you? You look positively worn out? Have you been busy running the most fabbest country in the world? Personally pulling those resources of all kinds out of the ground and fashioning them into food and goods for the people?'

'Erm ... Oh, yes. Quite so.'

'I bet you're working flat out and completely selflessly to establish a workers utopia that will be the envy of the planet — of all planets!'

'Oh, indeed. Yes, I've been at it, all right.'

'You know, when America and Europe and everyone else gets to see what a fab job you've done there and how happy and contented and well fed and provided for the people are, I shouldn't be surprised there was a people's revolution here as well.'

'Really? I mean, of course, it is a matter of historical inevitability.'

'Oh, yes, they'll be rising up and locking up the capitalists, and then they'll be inviting you to run their countries for them, I shouldn't wonder.' Persephone managed to insert an entire bun in her mouth in one go.

'I, er, yes, it's ... the day's not far off.'

'I expect you've personally designed an intercontinental ballistic missile or two today as well, haven't you. I know you're awfully good at that sort of thing.'

'Oh, yes, one or two.' Kim's eyes were saucering at the spectacle of food and indulgence on his computer screen.

'And how are the unicorns?'

'They are well ... er ... What are you doing Mrs Gousset?'

'Oh, don't mind us. Just a little tiffin, you know. Helps us get through the task of finding poor old Victoria — my daughter. You know we're looking for her. We had a conversation about it a few days ago just before she disappeared for the umpteenth time. What a coincidence!'

'You did wh—' Hades tried, but Persephone bunged a huge cake in his hole before he could ruin the atmosphere.

'Oh, yes, everyone who helps us gets sticky buns. Lots and lots of sticky buns and lashings of tea.'

'Buns?'

'Yes, buns. Exactly like these buns here. But I'm sure this is all very boring for you. I expect a huge pile of buns like this is a quick snack for you between breakfast and brunch. I expect you're eating sticky buns like this in your sleep.'

'I expect I am.'

'I mean all those mountains in your country must be riddled with bun mines. You must have buns pouring out of them by the train load.'

'Train loads.'

'Sticky buns, sugared buns, glazed buns, cream buns, jam buns, buns with bits of crystallised fruit on them, chocolate-covered buns, buns with banana in them, marmalade buns, strawberry buns, buns with so much icing sugar on you need a bunker buster to get through to the bunny bit underneath; walnut buns, cinnamon buns, custard buns, buns steeped in maple syrup, buns with fresh slices of apple or burned orange ...'

'How many buns do people get?'

'I beg your pardon?'

'The people who help you. How many buns do they get?'

'Oh, just for helping they get all the buns they can eat. Isn't that right?' she asked everyone at the table.

'Mwum mwumm mwummmmm,' they all agreed.

'And I suppose that if anyone gave us any information that actually led us to finding Victoria, well, they'd probably get whole boat loads of buns. Enough buns to feed an entire nation with enough buns left over to gorge themselves silly pretty indefinitely, I shouldn't wonder. I imagine any hypothetical leader would look fairly god-like in the eyes of his population if it suddenly came to a national bun free-for-all. But you can't possibly be interested in our inferior buns when your own country is awash in superior buns. I've heard that North Korean buns are made from pebbles. Yum! You must invite us over for tea sometime.'

'My interest in buns is purely ... academic and scientific, you understand. We would like to study western buns to determine how long people can keep eating such things before historical necessity takes its course and your decadent cultures collapse.'

'But I thought the unicorns told you all that.'

'They do but they enjoy — academically — seeing their predictions repeated in nature.'

'Well, I do believe the United States is at this moment, as we speak as it were, stuffing all eleven of its aircraft carriers with buns against such a hypothetical contingency.'

'How soon could they be ... somewhere.'

'Somewhere hypothetical?'

'A hypothetical somewhere, to be more precise.'

The US secretary of state leaned in and whispered in Persephone's ear.

Teasing out fragments of bun the secretary of state had left in her ear after whispering in it, Persephone told Kim 'By a complete and utter coincidence, all eleven bun-laden carriers are bobbing in the Yellow Sea, not twenty minutes from your port of Nampho. They could be a hypothetical somewhere tonight.'

'The Fortress of Alamut, but it wasn't me that told you. And these had better be straight-up buns or there will be nuclear war.'

Kim clicked off.

'You heard the man,' shouted Persephone. 'The Fortress of Alamut! To your horses everyone!'

'Do I have time for just one more bun?' asked Hades.

61

Seamus woke up on the cold, earthy floor of the corridor. It was dark, absolutely dark. He was in pain. The hurt centred in his loins and spread out thickly from there to every other part of his body. There was so much pain emanating from his balls, it was probably oozing into the floor and the walls and causing them to hurt too.

He tried to stand, which caused him more pain. He assumed there was a problem with his underpants to be suffering this much pain but attempting to adjust them, he found that he had no pants. He was in his bare bottom. Birthday-clad from the waist down.

Climbing to his feet caused pain like another physical assault to his nethers. He clung to the wall and stood and swayed a moment before shuffling off. In the blackness, he stumbled on something large, which gave a muffled fart.

He didn't know what it was and didn't want to know and got away as fast as his agony would let him.

His ears peered around in the dark but found nothing. There was no gunfire, no voices, no tap dancing. He had no idea whether that was a good thing or a bad thing.

When he stumbled into the main hall, the Hashishin were gathered on the hospitality carpets, grim faced, silent and smoking up a major smog alert.

'Jesus Christ, give me a bang on one of those! What hasn't happened to me today?'

'What hasn't happened to all of us, Seamus?' It was Billy that had spoken but the sentiment clearly came from the Hashishin as a group.

'You didn't say anything about firefights. We could have been killed,' someone added.

'Sorry about that. But what about me? I've just been duffed up by that Gousset lass. I feel like my balls have exited through my ears.'

'Yeah, where is she?'

'Oh, she's escaped. When I've got this inside me, we'll be off after her.'

'Well, see you then.'

'Will you not be after her with me?'

'No, we'll not be after her with you, Seamus,' said Billy.

Another red-eyed, shaggy faced member added, 'Let's be straight about this, Seamus. When we came down here you didn't say we'd have to be doing anything, now. In fact, I thought the whole point of this Hash Republic, the Spliffate, the Puffate, whatever you want to call it, was so to get away from doing things.'

'Absolutely,' said another. 'Given the choice between, one, shooting it out with North Korea's finest, two, running across the hot desert looking for a stray totty, and three, sitting comfortably on my arse with a doobie in my face, guess which I'll be choosing.'

Seamus had to concede a point. But only a bit. 'Well, put like that, you have a compelling argument. But think what her underpants could do for us. Automated everything, like. We wouldn't have to lift a finger.'

'Ah, well, it's that lifting the finger thing that's bothering me. I thought the point of the Spliffate was that there would be nothing to lift a finger for.'

'You haven't taken a shine to her, have you now, Seamus? Cos that's another thing I thought the Spliffate was about — freedom from distracting desires, leaving us free for the way of the spliff.'

'Aye, you toke the high way and I'll toke the low way, and I'll be insensible afore ye.'

'That's so beautiful. You're bringing tears to my eyes, so you are.'

'So, what's the plan, then, Seamus?'

Seamus needed to quell this swell of sulkiness that passed for a rebellion in the ranks. 'Well, I reckon we've got the nuke and no one will touch us while we have that, so we'll sit here and think of nothing to do.'

But deep down in the fog of hash, Seamus knew he was going to have to get off his bum and go after Victoria.

'And Seamus, did you know you've got a bare bottom, now? What happened to your underpants?'

62

Kim Il-bond recovered consciousness. His training as a spy helped him with that — mental tricks; visualising. Visualising yourself climbing up a ladder from a deep well up toward the light of the outside world was one option. Walking a garden path to your grandmother's house where a special scrummy tea was waiting was a more peaceful alternative. Screaming through the sky like a Valkyrie on your way to murder the bloke who made you unconscious was yet another choice, and the one that Kim preferred.

His military training didn't help him with the pair of sweaty, unwashed underpants wrapped round his head threatening to choke him. He had to wrestle with those in a very unmilitary, very appalled and disgusted kind of way.

They reeked of sweat and hashish and all the other things long-unwashed underpants tend to reek of.

Hash.

They must belong to one of the Hashishin. They might belong to Seamus i-Sabbah himself. It was Seamus he was pursuing when he was ambushed. It made sense that it was Seamus that ambushed Kim. With his own underpants.

Damn it! He nearly took the name of the Fandoobly Leader in vain, but checked himself just in time.

How long had he been unconscious? Where might Seamus now be with the girl? Kim groaned. Not only had he apparently lost The Absolutely Most Fantasticest Leader's vital military asset — viz, Victoria's expertise in martial foundation wear — but had at the same time lost His Extreme Bumptiousness's newest shag-to-be.

It was the re-education camp for Kim, and he quite deserved it.

'I have shamed my country. I have shamed my leader. I have shamed myself.' He stifled a sob and unholstered his pistol. He clicked off the safety and drew the bolt to cock it and very carefully fired a full magazine into Seamus's underpants on the floor.

Kim headed off to find his men and a way to get Victoria back.

Back on the roof he paused to take stock. The helicopter seemed to be full of bullet holes, which his men were attempting to stopper with gobs of chewed earth and corks and bits of rag.

'Will it fly?'

'Not without a rat, it won't,' the pilot told him.

'A rat? Are we back to that? We had five rats a while ago.'

'Dead.'

'Caught in the crossfire?'

'No. They were already dead.'

'But we saw them moving moving. One of them was break dancing.'

The pilot held up a rat by its tail and and a pair of clockwork false teeth. 'The rats had been tampered with. They seem to have been temporarily animated by use of this crude mechanical device, one of which was inserted into each rat. We were duped.'

'Duped. Well. We'll see about that. No one dupes the agents of the Democratic People's Republic of Korea and then goes on to tittle-tattle about it. Let's make some holes in people on behalf of Our Supremely Super Duper Leader. I am totally pissed off, and no one does totally pissed off like a Korean.'

Expertly clicking and clacking the bolts and levers on the biggest of his guns Kim set off in search of Seamus and Victoria.

63

Seamus, meanwhile, was doggedly pursuing Victoria after just one more toke, and he was smack in the middle of that when Kim stormed in.

The commando hurled the dirty, bullet-riddled underpants at Seamus. 'Are these yours?'

'Oh man, I was so wondering where these had got to.' He put them on. In their current murdered state they were futile as underthings or anything for that matter. If you had tried to recycle them as a rag to polish your shoes, the shoes would have slipped right through them.

'Where did you find them?'

'They were on my head trying to kill me, where I presume you put them.'

'They were on your head trying to kill you? My undies? That's not something you would normally tell people, mate.'

'You ambushed me! In the dark! With those pants! And you tricked me with the rats!' Kim bellowed.

'That's not something most people would shout about, either' Billy giggled. 'You're full of the revelations today aren't you.'

'Where's the woman? You kidnapped her. I saw her on your shoulder.'

'I kidnapped her? That's rich! And she was following you around because she liked you?'

'She belongs to our extraordinarily gorgeous leader. She is promised to him. It is an honour for her to submit to him.'

'Oh, I think she might have her own ideas about that. Eh, lads?'

Snigger.

'Oh, God, not the sniggering thing again. What is it with the sniggering? It's like talking to a bunch of retarded nine-year-olds.'

Seamus and his people thought this was worth another good snigger and a bit of a splutter too.

'OK. Where's the girl? I demand the girl. The girl's not yours.'

'I'm afraid that the girl has a mind of her own and I don't know where she is now. Could be anywhere in Alamut. Could be outside. I was just looking for her as a matter of fact.'

Seamus was peering at the glowing end of his joint as if he might find her in there.

'She was with you. You had her. How did you lose her?'

Seamus looked haunted.

'She, er, kind of got away, OK. Does it matter how? I was not prepared for that particular manoeuvre. I didn't consider it an option so I didn't belt up tight.'

'Jesus Christ, man,' spluttered Billy. 'The lass gave Seamus a wedgie. That's hilarious!'

'Hey, Seamus is that how your pants ended up on Kim-boy here? She wedgied your knickers right on to his head? Oh, that's priceless!'

'No,' said Seamus and Kim together. 'That's not what happened! Probably.'

'Oh that wee slip of a lass duffed up two big, gun-carrying men with their own underpants. Oh, that's class!'

'Look,' burst Kim. 'She did not attack me with my underwear. She attacked me ... with ...'

'Yes! Another man's underwear. Oh, far out!'

Kim fired a burst from his machine gun into the ceiling, which had the effect of momentarily shutting up the guffawing Hashishin. It also had the effect of bringing down a number of suddenly dead bats on Kim's head, which set off the Hashishin all over again.

Kim's next burst might have been right at the hash fundamentalists but for a sudden shaking and thundering that seized Fortress Alamut. To say that shaking and thundering had seized Alamut was a complete and utter understatement; a statement that was so under it was singed by the fire at the Earth's core. It felt that a very stroppy, red, shaggy, underlord had stepped up from that fiery realm and grabbed Alamut to give it a good rattling. Why underlords, red or shaggy or otherwise, would want to rise up from their fiery seats just to rattle things is not known. I don't suppose we ever think to ask when it happens.

It was just dawning on the denizens of Alamut that this was not any old underlord, but the Lord of the Undies, Sir Hades Gousset himself, when dozens of black-clad, gun-wielding men rappelled into the hall. The doors burst open to admit more of the same.

The Special Air Service, Navy SEALs, Brigade des Forces Spéciales Terre, KSK Kommando Spezialkräfte, the collected coast guards of every country that had a coast to guard, the mountain rescue teams of every country that had a mountain to rescue, filled the air, the walls, the doors, the floors, the closet and the loos and probably the pantry shelves too.

Kim's gang and Seamus's mob were faced with the options of fighting it out against vastly superior numbers and expiring in a hail of bullets or of politely asking the newcomers, 'Can we help you?'

Billy of the Hashishin wondered to whom he should first offer a spliff. 'Anyone want a bang on this number?'

'What have you done with our daughter?' Sir Hades and Persephone pushed through the throng to take charge.

'And your daughter would be ...?'

'Missing! That's what our daughter would be. And you lot have her stashed here somewhere.'

'If she's missing we can't have her. If we had her, she

wouldn't be missing, would she.' Seamus's reasoning failed to impress the guests.

'Have you,' Kim asked warily, 'tried putting her image on milk cartons?'

'Don't make fun of me, Sonny Jim,' bawled Hades.

'Now, you say she's missing. That's a very general description. Could you, sort of, narrow it down a bit?'

'Her name is Victoria Gousset, daughter of Hades and Persephone Gousset,' said Hades as if it were some kind of death threat, which, in a way, it was.

'Oh, her! You just missed her,' said Seamus tiredly. 'I think she just stepped out for some air. To be sure, she'll be back in a minute. Come to think of it, if you run now, you might catch her. I wouldn't be hanging round here wasting any more time, though.'

'You expect me to believe that she's not here?'

'It would be very helpful if you did.'

'I don't feel very obliging, I'm afraid. I feel more ... I dunno ... like dismantling each of you, one at a time with pliers and a screwdriver and a blunt and rusty hacksaw until one of you tells me what I want to know.'

'And if we don't know anything?'

'Then your remains will get a proper burial instead of being left to the rats.' Hades turned to Kim. 'How about you? You look like a man of honour. Judging by your insignia, you are of the Democratic People's Republic of Korea's own department of dirty tricks — kidnapping, sabotage, espionage, ice cream buying, and brandy procuring. In fact, you look like the man who took her from Switzerland. My mistake. You're not a man of honour, you're a lowlife snatcher of helpless young women and no better than this bunch of dirtbags here.'

Kim bristled at being compared to the Hashishin. 'I was delivering your daughter to veneration and glory. I last saw her on the shoulder of this one here —' gesturing at Seamus, 'as he disappeared like a rat into the bowels of this place. That woman,' he continued, 'is the property of Our Unbelievably Effulgent Leader and —' and he didn't get to finish his sentence because Hades' punch sent Kim and his special training straight to the floor.

'Property? My daughter? OK, Hilda, get me my pliers and screwdriver and rusty old hacksaw. We'll start on him as soon as he wakes up.'

'My I suggest fetching also your old hand-cranked whisk? We've found that very useful in the past.'

'Ooh, you mean the one with the rickety whisk blades? The one that wobbles when you turn the crank no matter how hard you try to hold it steady?'

'The very one.'

'Oh, yes, by Jove. Do fetch that in. It's quite good on eyelids, isn't it.'

'It's *very* good on eyelids. I'll be right back.'

'Right then, sonny Jim.'

'My name's not sonny Jim. My name's Seamus. Seamus i-Sabbah.'

'Right then sonny Seamus i-Sabbah. Where's my daughter?'

'She really has escaped,' affirmed Billy, not wanting to be witness to any splattery blood scenes that would disturb his buzz.

'Hilda will be back with the whisk in a jiffy. You'll have to do better than that. Convince me. How, for example did one woman escape dozens of heavily armed men in a squatty little hole in the ground like this?'

Seamus buried his face in his hands.

'Well?'

Hilda appeared at his side clattering the whisk as she wound the handle.

'Well?' asked Persephone. 'That's a very impatient whisk if memory serves. It likes to quickly get going on the job.'

'But takes its time and does it properly once it's started,' Hades clarified.

'Argh!' groaned Seamus.

'Erm,' said Billy, 'what he's trying to say, or trying not to say, is that she pulled a wedgie on him.'

'A wedgie!' exclaimed Hades and Persephone.

'Is that right, sonny Sabbath, or whatever your name

is?'

'Argh!' confirmed Seamus.

Billy continued to elucidate for his stricken comrade. 'And then she apparently nicked his knickers and overpowered Kim with them — Kim being the one piled on the floor there in an untidy heap.'

'My daughter overpowered two men with one pair of underpants?' said Hades.

'Only a Gousset could do that,' said Persephone

'I'm so proud,'

'I'm going to cry.'

'We're all going to cry,' said Hilda.

When Persephone and Hades and Hilda Titanium and Catshit and the SAS and the SEALs and Brigade des Forces Spéciales Terre, KSK Kommando Spezialkräfte, the various coast guards and mountain rescue teams and boy scouts and the brandy-carrying St Bernard and uncle Tom Cobbly, who had wandered in sensing a crowd to be made up, had all sniffled and snuffled into their handkerchiefs a good bit, Persephone asked, 'And where does one go when one escapes around here?'

'Argh!' said Seamus.

'The desert,' translated Billy.

'And is that near here?' asked Persephone.

'Ah. It rather *is* here,' said Hades without any joy in his voice in narrowing down the whereabouts of his daughter.

'For miles and miles around. In every direction,' amplified Billy.

'And where does one go when one is in the desert? How does one get out?'

'Now. We don't have too many deserts in Essex where I grew up,' observed Hades, 'but I think the point of them is, once you are in, the only way out is rescue.'

He looked around the hall that was crowded with every kind of survival expert you could think of.

'Am I wrong?'

'No, you're not wrong,' answered several hundred people in unison.'

'So ...' ventured Catshit, 'that means ...'

'Yes,' encouraged Hilda.

'That ...'

'Yes,' encouraged Persephone.

'That ...'

'Yes,' encouraged Hades.

'That ... I should go and lie down with the rhubarb again,' concluded Catshit.

'Absolutely,' agreed Hilda.

'And while you're doing that, we'll arrange to rescue my daughter,' said Hades. 'We'll quarter the area. The French can take the north, the Americans the west, the British the east, and the St. Bernard the south. Is the dog going to be all right in that coat? Perhaps I should relieve him of some of the weight of that brandy.'

All the while there had been some coming and going around the US secretary of state with staff whispering in his ear and muttering into sleeve cuffs and lapel pins.

'Sir Hades,' he hailed. 'I'm told we have an ongoing issue thing situation ongoing here.'

'Yes, I'm trying to find my missing daughter.'

The secretary of state took another consultation. 'Yes, sir, this would seem to an alternate ongoing issue situation in addition to the concurrent issue circumstance you reference.'

'I only have one daughter. I can't be looking for two.'

The secretary of state look puzzled and took some more advisement.

'Gee, that advisement tastes good. We've got cases of the stuff. Would you like to try a bottle?'

'Does it have brandy in it? I'm rather averse to things that don't have brandy in them.'

'Now, it seems we have radar contacts suggesting several military-style fleets of helicopters and ground forces, all with fighter support heading this way.'

'Good Lord! What does it mean?'

'It means that there's a lot of helicopters, ground forces and fighters, heading this way.'

'Good Lord again! Who is it?'

'Well, judging from the radar profiles and vectors it's

everyone who isn't already here. We seem to have task forces from Iran, Russia, China, India, Pakistan, Israel, and, er, the rest of the world, closing in on us at high velocity.'

'What do they want?'

'What does anyone want? Underpants. That's pretty hot intellectual property you've got in your trousers there.'

'I wouldn't want it to fall into the wrong hands.'

'Quite so, but we have a contingency plan for just this contingency.'

'Fabulous. And what's that?'

'We are going to fight them off with our massive military might and our even bigger sense of entitlement and start a world war in the process.'

'Where's that dog with the brandy? How far away are they?'

'We're here!' said a very smart military man striding through the main doors.

'Here!' said another very smart military man striding through a different set of doors.

'Here!' yet another striding through a window.

'Here!' This one came from the loo and was wearing scuba gear.

'Here!'

'Here!'

'Here!'

'Here!'

'Here!'

For the second time in under an hour the doors and windows of Alamut dramatically thronged with men who were specially trained in dramatically thronging doors and windows while wearing black. Given that the hall of Alamut was already unreasonably crowded, this caused a lot of unseemly pushing and shoving which of its own could have started a global war before anyone had got as far as underwear-security-related issues.

'OK,' bellowed Hades. 'I think we have the idea.' Turning to the particularly smart fellow who was the first. 'So who are you?'

'Shut up! I ask the questions around here. I am Colonel Ahmediflibbertygibbetydad of the Iranian Revolutionary Guard. You, Hades Gousset, are under arrest for being in Iran with a very large and hostile military task force, being in possession in Iran of an alcohol-laden dog — disgusting in every way — and of not having the proper entry visa. Do you have the secret military underpants designs on you? Not that they have anything to do with the reasons we are arresting you.'

'Hold on a moment. I am General Wodka of the special Stoli commandos, and this man is my prisoner.'

'Why is he your prisoner? He's in my country.'

'I'm extraditing him. He is a unique threat to the security of Russia and it is my duty to take him to Guantanomoski, in Siberia for good Russian cabbage soup and this has nothing to do with military secret underpants, oh no, not a bit.'

'I almost agree with the good Generalski, but it is China that is specially threatened by the terrible underthings that this man has set loose in this world, and so I am extraditing him and thoughts of getting our hands on his secret technologies couldn't be further from our noble minds.'

'Oh, yeah?' said a gentleman wearing the insignia of Israel's special forces. 'Well, my helicopter is parked right behind yours, so you're not going anywhere. You can leave Gousset with me and we'll lock him away where his underpants secrets are safe with us — I mean where he can't be any further threat to the integrity of the state of Israel, whose integrity is way more important than all your integrities added together and multiplied by a large random number from the Kabbalah.'

The leaders of the contingents of all the other countries had something to say on the matter too, all at the same time and what they had to say was more or less the same thing, that they were each uniquely threatened by supposed underthings of mass destruction, on whose design they had no designs of their own, and were going to take the designer into custody.

They were all very adamant about it.

'Look, my country's bigger than your country and we have more nukes than you,' said the representative of Russia.

'Yeah? Well our nukes are better than yours so we don't need so many. And our country's better than yours so it doesn't need to be so big. Ha! Your big country is just a practice target for space rocks, anyway,' said the American secretary of state.

'What do they mean "threat to world security"? I am world security,' thought Hades. 'And how dare they bicker about my fate as if I were a chattel to be handed about?' He decided it was about time to bellow for order and put everyone straight, when someone else beat him to it.

'Listen the fuck up! Oi!'

Something in the voice compelled the bickering leaders to shut exactly the fuck up and listen. It was probably the note of hysterical, dangerous insanity that they found so compelling.

'Oh, yes, you are all wrong!' It was Seamus. 'Oh yes, hoo hoo ha ha hee hee woo hoo fnarr fnarr ding-dong dingly on high! Oh ho ho ho oh ho ho ho, you are sooooooooooo, sooooooooooo with dingly-dangly knobs on wrong wrong wrong! Cos I got da bomb! I got da bomb! I got da bomb!'

Seamus was on his feet clutching the silver cylinder: the nuke he had taken from Kim.

'Gibber, gibber, ha, ha, ha. Look at me, Mum, I'm on top of the world.'

'Bomb?' enquired Billy. 'Oh, the bomb.'

'OK, now I'm in charge and you all do what I say now. Got that?'

'Bomb?' enquired the several hundred people present who had not been party to the rat-for-nuke exchange earlier in the day.

'Bomb?' enquired the Hashishin. 'Do we have to do anything?'

'Erm, Seamus, there's something I need to tell you about the bomb.'

Seamus was not about to listen to Billy. He was a man whose moment had come, prematurely drunk on victory and unhinged at the imminence of unlimited power and the establishment of his life dream of a spliffy, puffy paradise on Earth, not to mention revenge for undies-induced humiliation.

'Yes, the bomb. The bomb that goes boom. Boom ba-da-boom-bada-boom.'

'About that bomb, Seamus.'

'Is that man saying he has a nuclear weapon?' asked Hades.

'Watch my lips daddio, that's it in a nutty nutshell entirely what I'm saying exactly. Hee hee hee.'

'Is he going to let off the bomb?' asked Catshit.

'Do we have to do anything?' worried the Hashishin some more.

'About that bomb, Seamus.'

'Yes, the actual bomby-bomby-bomb-bomb. So back off or it's bye bye boogaloo for you.'

'You do realise, don't you, young man —'

'Don't call me young man! Don't you know who I am? I am Hassan i-Sabbah, the Old Man of the Mountain.'

'He's actually Seamus Dingle,' said Billy in an apologetic tone.

Hades stepped forward to confront Seamus. 'Very well. You do realise, don't you, young man, that if you detonate that bomb, you'll end up dead with the rest of us — you and your band of muddled men. Now, you look like a cowardly, snivelling wretch. Are you really ready for self immolation?'

'Why would it hurt me? It's *my* bomb! Does a mad dog bite its owner?'

'We are sooooooooooooo fucked,' said the American secretary of state, who knew a few things about nuclear weapons.

'About that bomb, Seamus.'

'No, you listen to me. I let this off and victory is mine. There'll be no more squares, right? No more nagging mums, no more bosses, no more prannies from the

JobCentre telling me to get a job or they cut me off, and no more pigs busting you for doing what you want. No more straights, man. Everyone will be free, you understand? Free and the spliffate will be established everywhere, and we'll be free to toke anytime, anywhere and stash will be free and compulsory.'

'And no more underpants, I shouldn't wonder,' put in Hades. 'They don't grow on trees, you know. Someone has to get up in the morning and make them.'

'Well, boo hoo to undies. I'll wear my swimmers instead.' Seamus held the silver cylinder above his head. 'So back off, you square-shaped grandaddy irrelevances. Or I blow you all to thingdom wotsit.'

'About that bomb, Seamus.'

'Oh, this is pure nonsense. You aren't about to do anything of the sort,' snapped Persephone.

'Oh, aren't I?' Seamus had just been goaded by a woman, his nemesis. 'Well, look, you know what? Why am I even giving you a chance? Why don't I let the thing off now and get rid of you all in one go? Why wait?'

'Now, look —'

'Are you going to succumb? Or are you going to kaboom?'

'Seamus?'

'We'll never give in to the likes of you, you waster. Get on with it!'

'Seamus?'

'Look ma! Top of the world! Bye-bye fool world! Ha ha ha! Be it on your head!'

And Seamus, brandishing the bomb aloft gave the top a decisive twist. A thick brown liquid glooped out over his head.

'Well, be it on your head,' guffawed Hades amid the general hilarity in the hall.

'What is this?' screamed Seamus.

'Mulligatawny soup,' said Billy. 'I was trying to tell you.'

'Mulligatawny soup?'

'Oh aye. After the shooting, while you were away, I

took at look at the bomb. I'd never seen a bomb before. Actually, I thought it looked like an ordinary thermos so I unscrewed the lid and it was an ordinary thermos. It was empty, so I heated up some Mulligatawny and put it in there. Soup always tastes nicer out of a thermos, haven't you noticed?'

'Oh, for crap's sake,' said a deflated Seamus. 'Anyone got a doobie? That's me done for today. Over to you, Daddio.'

64

Seamus plonked down on the hospitality rug and accepted a joint from the Hashishin who took this turn as a signal to smoke their way out of this predicament and off the planet.

But the ordeal was not over for anyone. Not by a long way.

'Right,' said Colonel Ahmediflibbertygibbetydad. 'Where were we?'

'Mutually assured destruction,' assured the Secretary of State.

'Oh yes, custody of the old pants man.'

'Well, look here, buddies,' the Secretary of State went on, 'I just put the armed forces of my country on full nuclear alert so you can just behave and be off now.'

China was not impressed. 'Oh, yeah, well, I put my nukes on alert before you put your nukes on alert.'

'So what? Our nukes are faster than anyone's nukes, so it doesn't matter how many times you put yourself on alert. You're toast.'

'Big deal. Our nukes are smarter and wilier than your nukes so, you don't impress me.'

'Well, I'm sorry but our nuclear forces are so badass, they'll trump all your nuclear forces put together if it comes to a night of painting the town holocaust red.'

Hades had his own war to finish. He bore down on Seamus all fumes and fury.

'Right now that we've got that little bid for world domination out of the way, tell me what you've done with my daughter.'

'Seriously, man, she's gone. She's outta here.'

Hades fixed his most sulphuric interrogatory eye on the Hashishin who glumly nodded their confirmation. He attached the same eye on Kim's men, who gave him the same message.

'Oh buggery bugger-bags,' announced Hades.

Persephone was at his side. 'Hades. Do something. If these dolts have their way there will be no world and our daughter and everyone else will be lost forever.'

'Look, I have the button.' The secretary of state was holding aloft a device. 'One press of the button here, and our entire nuclear fleet is launched from home.'

'Well, same here. One word from my and my country will rain fire on your country.'

'Not so fast, I also have the button, and it's bigger and redder and more important than any of your buttons.'

These announcements produced renewed and redoubled shouting of 'Hubbub! Hubbub!'

Hades wondered whether he could reasonably strong-arm everyone with a button before any one of them could set off Armageddon.

65

As Hades was wondering who to hurl himself at first, the secretary of state shouted, 'Right. That's it. Don't say I didn't warn you.' Holding aloft his nuclear button so everyone could see, he pressed it.

Immediately, Russia, China, the UK, France, India, Pakistan, and Israel all did the same.

The sun went out.

This was quite striking. The hall became still. The delegates of the world's most powerful militaries all wondered whether ordering a nuclear strike, world annihilating as it might be, would turn the sun off too. And perhaps — let us hope — reflected a moment on what they were doing to the world by ordering a nuclear war. A nuclear war over underpants.

Someone farted.

Hades, being an alert sort of chap — and you don't become the most important man in the world without being an alert sort of chap — noticed, that not only had the sun gone out, but that the flaming torches and candles that aided the natural light in the hall had gone out too. As had the displays and power lights on all the various electrical bits and bobs that everyone was carrying.

'This could mean that something odd is happening,' said Hades in his best calm and in-charge voice, which other than furiously angry was the only voice he had.

'Oh, good,' said Hilda. 'The day wasn't sufficiently interesting.'

Then came the thrumming. The earlier shaking and hellish cacophony that accompanied Hades' arrival had at least sounded like helicopters once you thought about it. This thrumming was something altogether odder and more sinister.

This thrumming came from everywhere all at once. It came from the sky, it came from the earth, it came from the walls of rock; it came from inside you, it came from your tum, it came from your feet and most alarmingly or most thrillingly, depending what your attitude is to mind bending experiences, it came from inside your head.

'Definitely, something odd,' affirmed Hades.

'What trickery is this?' demanded the Iranian attache in the dark.

'Yes, someone is doing trickery-pokery. I demand to know who it is and I demand that they stop right away!' said China.

'Well, I'm not doing trickery-pokery. How do I know it isn't you doing trickery-pokery?'

'If someone doesn't stop this trickery-pokery right now, I'm pressing my button again.'

'If you press your button again, I'm pressing my button again.'

'Not if I press my button again first!'

Light burst in from the windows in hard, angled beams of titanium. If someone had turned the sun back on, they had first towed it to a point a few metres above the fortress.

'Right that's it! I've had enough! I've pressed my button again.'

'You can't have because I have.'

'You're both wrong I pressed my button again so you can jolly well desist with whatever you've done.'

'I'm pressing my button again and again and again as hard as I can but nothing is happening!'

'It's the trickery-pokery!'

'Oh, wail!'

There was a loud pop and and liquid quicksilver poured out of a hole in space right above them and pooled in mid air into the shape of a large luminous egg, which in turn went shhhhhhhfpt! and opened like an expensive executive toy, layers of shimmering silver shell sliding back into each other. The silver shell cradled an oval of shimmering black and the oval of shimmering black cradled a human figure. The human figure swept one hand through the air and all the military nuclear launch devices and communication doohickies and guns and weapons and what have you leapt from the hands of all the military personnel in the hall, into the air, where it hurtled into the same hole in space-time from which the egg had appeared, turning to liquid as it exited this dimension. It was as if the human figure with that one wave of the arm had swept all the weapons and bomb launchers out of the hall.

'Victoria! What on earth are you doing?' demanded Persephone. 'And you've coloured your hair!'

'I'm depriving these boys of their toys before they blow up the planet,' said Victoria. 'I blocked the launch signals for the nuclear missiles, so the world is safe for the time being. Hi, Mum. Hi, Dad. Hilda. Everyone. I saw Catshit outside. Is he here with you? You may want to do something with him. He's giving the rhubarb a really hard time. Oh, hi, Seamus. You still here? Sorry about the huge wedgie thing, but you were making off with me on your shoulder against my will. I hope I didn't humiliate you too much. And Kim too. I'm sure that being asphyxiated with Seamus's briefs wasn't the best thing that ever happened to you ... oh, where is Kim?'

Kim's men pointed to the crumpled heap at their feet.

'Oh, Daddy hit you, did he? Well, that's nice.'

'But how did you get up there? Where have you been?' asked Hades.

'We've been looking all over for you. The armed forces of almost the entire planet have mobilised looking for you,' said Persephone.

'Ah, well, that's the thing. I wasn't on this planet, so you would have been looking for me in the wrong place wherever you looked.'

'You weren't on this planet? Have you been taking mushrooms?'

'No, honestly! I met these terribly nice aliens. Or rather they met me. Well, they picked me up. I was lost in the desert and not doing terribly well when they came down in their beautiful ship, oh, you should have seen it.'

'Aliens?' asked Persephone. 'You mean you had an alien abduction?'

'Oh, sort of, I suppose,' said Victoria brightly.

Hades was bothered by the mention of an alien ship. Was it space-worthy? Was the tax and insurance properly paid up? In short, was it good enough for his daughter. 'So, is this egg thing the space ship? Looks terribly frail and, er, small and perhaps someone is having you on.'

'Oh, no, this isn't the ship. I'm standing in an aperture in space-time created by the ship, which is hovering just over Alamut and blocking out the sun.'

Seamus was intrigued. 'Alien abduction? You mean with probes and all that?' he asked.

Victoria flushed. 'Oh, yes. The probes. Well, space is full of fascinating things, as it turns out. We've been round the block a few times already. I've seen the Crab Nebula. Had a fantastic seafood pasta there.'

'So they used probes on you,' Seamus insisted.

'Young man, I'm warning you,' said Hades warningly.

'Um. There were probes,' said Victoria flushing even more. 'On the ship. And then we zoomed by Alpha Centauri, because, you know, it's quite close in cosmic terms, just 4.2 light years.'

'So there were probes, and what exactly did they aaaaaaagh!'

Hades intervened in the probe theme and for the second time in one day Seamus suffered the indignity of a wedgie, this one terminating — *splat!* — in an infamous Hades kiss delivered by Hades' own forehead to the bridge of Seamus's nose while he was suspended above the floor, legs flailing helplessly, suspended in his own underthings.

Seamus forgot about the probes. He forgot about

everything as he joined Kim on the floor.

'Oh, I don't mind talking about the probes, Daddy. They're all part of the cosmic experience.'

'I mind, Victoria. And so will those bloody aliens when I get my hands on them.'

'Are you sure they're aliens, Victoria? There are a lot of strange people about who enjoy telling stories so they can take advantage of young women.'

'Oh, I do think they might be aliens, Mummy. They are silver and have been whisking me around the Milky Way and they have lights on the ends of their fingers — especially after picking their noses.'

'But they kidnapped you, Victoria. They ... they ... I don't know what they did, but you said they kidnapped you.'

'Well, they might have kidnapped me a bit at first. But think on this: I was lost on a desert road at night because I was trying to get away from these fools. No one knew I was there. I could have fallen into a hole, or been bitten by a snake or been seized by bandits or died of thirst —'

'Or been kidnapped by aliens,' pressed Hades.

'Oh, Daddy, they rescued me. I had already been kidnapped by umpteen people — including, as it turned out, you and Mummy, my own parents —'

Hades and Persephone looked at the floor and shuffled their feet around a bit.

'These people who aren't even strictly people took pity on someone who was not of their own kind and whisked me from probable death. As far as I can see, all the people who are supposed to be of the same species as me set about scheming to catch either me or my father for our knowledge of underthings. And then when you couldn't get what you wanted you all tried to blow up the world. Don't you think that's extraordinarily daft? Well, as far as I'm concerned, all I've had from people is people wanting to own me and control me, which is why I pulled my little stunt in the first place. I'm a person, not a thing to be handed about for your convenience like a bit of furniture.'

Hades drew himself up straight. 'Yes, I owe you an

apology. I have had this conversation with your mother. It has become apparent to me that while I thought I was giving you the best possible upbringing and giving you everything you want, I was in fact trying to bring you up to be something I wanted you to be: a pliant, obedient little girl who embodied my view of the world and the way I thought people ought to be. In doing this I overlooked and nearly lost the real Victoria. I apologise without reserve.'

'And so do I, Victoria!' exclaimed Persephone. 'I am so, so sorry!'

'Oh, Mummy! Oh, Daddy! And this has been a learning experience for me too. See: I was blond and now I'm brunette. Yes, it was silly and selfish of my to kidnap myself and cause all this trouble. I didn't know what I was doing. I now know that there were other ways to deal with my problems, and the irony is, I had to make that huge mistake to learn what those other ways were. I'm sorry, Mummy. I'm sorry, Daddy!'

'Oh, Victoria! We're just glad you're safe.'

Hades turned to the hall sopping tears from his face with the end of his beard. 'You may also apologise to my daughter.'

'Fine,' said Colonel Ahmediflibbertygibbetydad. 'Sorry. Now you and your secret underpants are coming with me.'

Chaos, once again, captured the hall.

66

The upper reaches of the main hall of Alamut, formed of the jut of huge slabs of granite were permanently lost in blackness. Even during the day when light entered by lower windows, nothing penetrated that lofty cleft.

What was up there? What was it like up there? What history had those shadows capped? These were questions that might occur to the enquiring and idle mind with time to spare on the hospitality rugs below.

"Duh! Wot?" might be a question to occur to a less enquiring mind.

We know there are bats up there — fewer after Kim's impetuous outburst with his gun.

No one had ever been observed dusting up there, so we might reasonably infer the presence of dust. And we might reasonably speculate on the presence of spiders if the bats haven't eaten them all or they haven't been carelessly shot.

There are certainly lots of shadows and shadows mean mystery. Shadows are also handy for mischief-makers to hide in until they choose to be revealed.

As now, for example. While the throng of people in the hall was in the renewed hubbub of threats and competition, four lumps of shadow detached themselves from the greater mass of dark and descended with blurry speed right to the egg of shimmering black where Victoria stood. One of the shadows grabbed Victoria from behind and held a gun to her head. The other three shadows disappeared inside the egg shape and out of view.

'No, for God's sake don't do that! You don't know what you're doing!' yelled Victoria.

'Nobody move or the girl gets it!' said the shadowy figure with the gun. 'And shut up girl, or someone else gets it,' it added as an afterthought.

Out of sight inside the egg there was a lot of shouting and banging and clanging.

'What in blue blazes is going on!' roared Hades.

'Unhand her, you bastard!' bellowed Persephone.

The shadow man fired a shot at the nearest wall. The bullet pinged and whined as it ricocheted from one wall to another causing everyone except the shadow man to duck.

'Stop it! You're going to ruin everything!' insisted Victoria.

The shadow man fired another shot, which did pretty much the same as the first with the additional effect of making Victoria silent. His dark companions crowded back into view from the interior of the egg, now armed, it would appear with an arsenal of unlikely looking alien weapons, evil looking contraptions of material that was blacker than black or in some cases brighter than bling.

'OK. Now we've got the alien guns. Here we go. This is where things get real.'

'Gnash!' bellowed Hades.

'Grr!' hollered Hilda.

'Maul!' screamed Persephone.

'Flay!' they all yelled together.

'Hello,' said Maul. 'Sorry we were so long. Did you miss me?'

'No,' shouted everyone in the hall.

'OK, OK. Haven't you ever heard a rhetorical question before?'

'Now that I have everyone's attention,' said Gnash, who was holding an especially evil-looking lump of evil at Victoria's head. 'It occurs to me that I have nothing in particular to say. Shall we just take this ship and vamoose, comrades?' He asked his accomplices.

'Leave Victoria here! You don't need her and she's been through enough already.' Persephone was imploring and threatening at the same time.

'Nah. Thanks for sharing the thought, though.'

Hades inflated himself to his not inconsiderable fully inflated size. 'What do you want, you blaggards? And how do you hope to get away with this, whatever it is you are doing?'

Gnash made a theatrical show of thinking. 'What do we want? Well, let me see. We've got these wild alien guns. We've got this wild alien beautiful ship with its wild alien technology. We've got all the nuclear triggers you guys were carrying that Victoria beamed aboard the ship out of your hands, along with all your funky military communication devices. And we've got the daughter of the most important man in the world. So what do we want? Erm? Well, I reckon everything will do. We'll have the planet and everybody and everything on it. Only we don't need to ask or negotiate about any of that. We have just taken it all.'

'Over my dead body,' said Hades finding a bit more height and girth about him.

'Hades ...' warned Persephone.

'Unfortunate choice of words, Hades, old chap. I hold the alien death ray.'

'Well, smarty pants, I just happen to be wearing my alien-death-ray-repelling underpants today so you can't touch me.'

'Oh, right,' said Gnash with affected boredom and shot Hades, who went splat, his molecules flying off in all directions. And then there was nothing left of him, not even a stain on the hospitality rug.

After a moment's pause to take in what had just happened there was pandemonium in the hall, everyone running in circles and shoving everyone else.

'Hades!' screamed Persephone. She rushed the egg-orb but Hilda held her back.

Victoria tried to struggle free from Gnash but he just held her more firmly and pressed his gun to her head more aggressively.

'Well, time to be off. We have a world to claim. Oh, and the aliens already used this ship's electromagnetic pulse generator to disable all your helicopters and stuff when they arrived, so there's no point in trying to rush around raising the alarm. Not that it would do you any good anyway.' The egg shape closed in on itself and with a phhhht! disappeared.

67

The inside of the beautiful ship was beautiful. Everything from the floor to the walls to the furniture to the instrument consoles to the GUI on the computer screens to the coffee cups, wine bottles, canapés and tapas dishes that covered most flat surfaces was composed of clean, elegant lines that spoke of elegance and practicality all rolled into one. The lighting was tastefully subdued. There were paintings on the wall that might have been original Ben Nicholsons. It was a bit like walking into a comfy lounge that had been gene-spliced with both an Apple store and Ikea.

Even the aliens, of whom there were several, reclining comfortably on their tasteful chairs — even more tasteful than Ikea chairs — at their tasteful consoles. They were a very sophisticated shade of silver-grey and wore shimmering toga-like dress and each had a finger inserted in its nose.

'Right,' announced Gnash at the aliens. 'I assume you can understand English and if you can't I can give you the URL for Google Translate. Now, set a course for Washington DC.'

The aliens looked blankly at Gnash. Well, their eyes were probably blank all the time, being big and saucer-like and densely black.

'Washington DC,' repeated Gnash.

'You, know, the capital city of the country that has Roswell.'

The two aliens at the most impressive of the consoles shrugged at each other and swivelling in their chairs set to tapping their fingers into the monitor screens which rippled like water and flashed up bewildering hallucinations in the air above.

'Yibber yibber yibber nit,' said the one alien.

'Nit yibber yibber yibber,' replied his crewmate.

'Yibber yibber nit yibber yibber,' joined in a third, which drew a general murmur of assent.

'Yibber yibber nit yibber probes yibber nit,' said a fourth, which provoked general laughter.

'No talking now! Just fly this damn thing. And make it snappy.'

'And what are we going to do when we get to this Washington?' asked Maul. 'Are we going to eat it?'

'No,' said Grr, puzzled by the question.

'Are we going to nuclear it then? Vaporise it to little bits?'

'Only if all the people in charge of Washington and the world want us to.' Gnash and Grr grinned horribly.

'And I assume we'll know whether they want us to by the speed they give in to our demands,' surmised Flay.

'Absolutely,' said Grr.

'We are going to park this crate over the White House, because that's what the alien ships always do in the films. Everyone will understand what that's supposed to mean. We might melt the capitol a bit just to make sure the world gets the message and because we can. It's a shame to waste all the potential destructive force on this ship.'

'And once we have everyone's attention, we'll announce on all radio and TV channels simultaneously that the world is under new management and that it is the duty of all world citizens who want to live to visit a certain aromatherapy shop in Preston and spend their life savings there. Woohahahahaha!'

'And if they stand up against you, you evil swine?'

Maul and Flay were tying a resisting Victoria into a seat with silver alien wire and silver alien packing tape.

'Then we'll zap them,' said Gnash. 'The whole city. And then we'll try New York, London, Paris, Moscow or Beijing. I think they'll have the message by then and we won't be seeing any further trouble.'

'The world belongs to us.'

'Yibber yibber nit nit yibber.'

'Speak English!' Gnash waved his gun at the aliens, who again shrugged.

'Nit nit nit nit nit nit yibber flange.'

'What are you saying? Do you want your weird little heads shot off?'

'They are saying,' broke in Victoria, ' that they are just coming to a stop exactly fifty metres above the White House.'

'Why didn't they say that?'

'They did.'

'No they didn't they said "Nit nit nit nit nit nit yibber flange."'

'Yibber nit yibber nit.'

'He says he already said that.'

'OK, OK, OK!' Gnash was shouting. 'Now let's take over all TV and radio channels and the internet and everything and get broadcasting — and let's melt that Capitol while we're at it. No, I want to see that dome explode. Let's blow that dome!'

'That was very fast,' said Maul in a tone of awe and wonder. 'One minute we were in Iran and now we are in America.'

'It's a *beautiful* ship, you plonker.'

'There's nothing faster than a *beautiful* ship,' Flay assured Maul.

'How about a *very beautiful* ship. Might a *very beautiful* ship be faster than a beautiful ship? And how about a *ravishing* ship? How fast would that be?' Maul wanted to know before being distracted and transfixed by the holographic shapes hovering over the control consoles.

'Pretty,' he murmured as if in a dream. 'Pretty-pretty.' He reached into the shapes as if to touch them.

'Ow!' he said when the nearest alien slapped his hand.

'Yibber', said the alien.

'Nit!' Said the one sitting next to him.

'Aw,' said Maul. 'No fair!'

'They are saying,' translated Victoria, 'that you nearly

hit the short cut that would catapult us to Andromeda through the sub ether of the space time continuum and that the jolt would cause us to become a smear of sub atomic particles on 2.5 million light-years of empty space.'

'And why would that be a bad thing?' Maul asked.

Gnash was out of patience. 'Look, are we going to blow up this capitol dome thing or what?'

'Blow up the Capitol?' asked Flay breaking out of her customary icy stillness. 'I don't mean to sound like a cynic, but ... who cares? I mean how is killing all these legislators, all these sociopathic collectors of lobby money going to disturb anyone? If you get any reaction at all, people might give you a list of other hated public institutions to blow up. No one is going to be awed into subjugation.'

'Nibber yit,' said another alien peering into one of the holograms.

Victoria's voice was taut with fear and horror. 'Oh, no! You have to stop right now. He says his scanners are picking up within the Capitol strong traces of bubblegum, dental braces, acne, Twizzlers, carpet bags with cat prints and copious amounts of feline fur.'

Gnash, Grr, Maul and Flay all looked quite blank.

'Don't you see? The Capitol is full of guided tours of school kids and cat fanciers.'

Gnash, Grr, Maul and Flay all remained quite blank.

'You are about to kill a lot of innocent people besides the legislators. Not just innocent people but sweet innocent people.'

'Your point being?' Gnash wanted to know.

'Will they somehow dampen the explosion causing the destruction of the dome to be a less than spectacular event?' wondered Grr.

Victoria insisted, 'No. They're just innocent. And sweet.'

'Well, that's good surely. Their destruction will provide the fear and sympathy that killing the suits won't.' Gnash pointed his evil gun at Victoria's head and leered at the aliens.

Grr, Maul and Flay pointed their own guns at the aliens.

'Yibber yibber yibber nit yibber more probes nit yibber fertang.'

'Let's see them get out of this one,' crowed Gnash.

The aliens together cleared their throats, which may have been an odd coincidence or may have been a ploy a to cover the sound of the black, eggy portal opening up behind the hijackers of the beautiful ship.

'You might want to put down your toys and give yourselves up before you get hurt,' said Hades, who had just materialised out of thin air behind them.

Gnash, Grr, Maul and Flay looked at Hades and then back at the aliens and then at Hades and then back at the aliens.

'Eat zappy death!' exclaimed Gnash and fired another bolt of deadly alien energy right at Hades, who instantly upended himself. The bolt of energy bounced off Hades' bottom. Hades laughed and disappeared.

'What the?'

'Boo!'

Gnash, Grr, Maul and Flay turned as one and fired together, and again the energy bolts just seemed to bounce off Hades' raised posterior — which vanished again. Now he popped up on their left and vanished again as they fired, to pop up on their right before disappearing yet again.

Gnash and his gang formed a defensive circle to cover all angles and waved their guns about ready for Hades' next appearance.

One of the little silver men removed his finger from his nose and examined the tip, which glowed brightly and greenly. The alien stretched his hand toward Grr watching the glow very carefully. It then made a small flicking gesture as one might get rid of a crumb from one's sleeve. Too fast to see properly, Grr shot back and through the space-time wormhole. Thousands of kilometres away in the Fortress Alamut, Grr exited the other end of the wormhole, which had just reappeared in the main hall, and went splat on the facing wall and then thump on the floor below.

Hades voice from within the aperture: 'All yours, my dear, I think.' followed by the tumbling bodies of Maul and Flay, which Persephone caught. She banged their heads together and then began knotting their limbs like a pair of party balloons she was mangling into interesting shapes.

Even the representatives of the most hard-bitten dictators in the hall of Alamut winced.

'Back! Back!' Gnash had a gun in each hand and was waving them at Hades and the aliens. 'Put those fingers away or I'll shoot them off.'

The aliens, as was their way, shrugged and re-inserted their glowing fingers in their noses.

Gnash backed a bit further toward the bound Victoria. 'Gousset, I've still got your daughter, and while I have her, I am still in control aaaaaaaaaaagh!'

Of course, Victoria was only pretending to be bound. Hades had secretly freed her before revealing himself, and as soon as Gnash was in range, and for the second time in twenty-four hours, she had inserted her hands in a man's trousers and pulled a tremendous wedgie, one that lifted Gnash off the ground and rendered his face red and blue and green and yellow.

And that's how Victoria appeared back in the hall of Alamut with her very-much-alive father, dragging the writhing, screaming Gnash by his underthings.

68

When Persephone saw her husband, alive and intact, emerge from the wormhole she ceased tying Maul and Flay in ever tighter knots. She took in the sight of her spouse and threw the two tangled criminals at him as if they were a big ball or a very large and unlikely vase.

'What on earth happened to you? I saw you killed. I thought you were dead. I was beside myself.'

Hades ducked and Maul and Flay bounced off the rim of the wormhole and into the back of the hall with a blood-curdling scream.

'Hello, darling. Sorry about the subterfuge. It was the best way of getting the drop on Gnash and company with minimum loss of innocent blood. That it was jolly good fun is an incidental by-product.'

'But ...' demanded Persephone, which but was seconded by a general murmur of seconding throughout the hall.

'I did warn Gnash I was wearing my alien death ray repelling underpants. And so I was. I didn't tell him that the same underpants had invisibility and teleportation functions too. I was able to deflect Gnash's shot — which had it not been for this sub-trouser technology would certainly have seen me done and dusted — while simultaneously disappearing and transporting myself onto the bridge of the ship, where I waited until the gang were thoroughly distracted before making my move.'

'And, I might add,' added Victoria, saved positively hundreds of children and cat fanciers from certain and utter death. And on top of that, he generally saved the whole of humanity too.'

Resounding cheers battered the ancient dignity of Alamut's hall and sent the bats into a barnstorming frenzy.

Hades waved his hands around indicating that there was more to tell. 'I must, must, must mention the bravery of my daughter Victoria who even in this state of extremis kept cool calm and collected, bamboozled the villains and then pulled that magnificent incapacitating wedgie which won the day.'

There was more cheering and throwing around of hats.

'Ahem,' said someone behind Hades and the aliens shuffled up to the entrance of the wormhole.

'And, of course,' he said without missing a beat we must give our special thanks to the crew of the beautiful ship — the *beautiful* people of the beautiful ship.'

The aliens removed their fingers from their noses.

'We know you wouldn't have blasted the Capitol while it was full of children and cat lovers.'

The aliens shrugged.

'On behalf of all of planet Earth, I would like to express the thanks of all humanity for your crucial role in saving us from the clutches of Gnash and Grr and their associates. And especially for getting Grr to flick off, as it were.'

'Not a problem, pal. Glad to be part of the fun,' said the tallest, greyest of the aliens.

'You speak English? All the time you spoke English and you didn't let on?'

'Oh, yeah. Everyone in the universe speaks English. It's the universal language. But we weren't going to let on to those tossers so we just made up some rubbish.'

'Well, we'll be off in moment,' put in another of the aliens. 'But before we go, we'd like to make a special presentation to Victoria as a sort of memento of all the fun and learning experiences we've had together.'

'Oh, that's really not necessary,' blushed Victoria.

'Well, we're going to do it anyway. And here you are: your very own probe.' The alien held out to Victoria a large tubular object with dangling wires.

'What on Earth?' fumed Hades.

Victoria put her hands on his shoulders. 'It's OK, Daddy. You are not going to punch them. It's their way of being friendly and showing respect.'

'Respect?'

'You just have to learn that some people have different ways.'

Hades looked unconvinced for a moment, then relaxed.

'OK. Then two can play at that game. I have gifts for everyone here.'

Gifts? From the richest most important man in the world? The cheering was the loudest yet.

'Yes,' bellowed Hades. 'The sensible underpants are on me! Everyone gets their own pair of super sensible undies to take home today.'

The cheering stopped.

'Oh.' Hades deflated a bit. 'I see. Did I say underpants? Slip of the tongue. What I meant to say was everyone gets as many sticky buns as they can fit in their pockets.'

Now even the bats were cheering.

Victoria, hugging her probe, said a warm farewell to the aliens as the wormhole lowered her and her father to the floor of the hall.

The link to the alien ship disappeared, and taking her parents by the arms, Victoria asked, 'Can we go home now? I miss my own bed.'

69

Hades' topiary was joining in splendidly with the party.

The bushes danced, drank, ate, told jokes, mingled and cavorted with most uninhibited and extrovert of the guests. You would not have guessed that just the day before they had been images of Hell inspired by Hieronymus Bosch. Quickly trimmed and re-tasked, they took on their new role of frolicking Bacchanalian satyrs with gusto and a number of poses that wouldn't be permitted in other circumstances.

Around the topiary mingled less bushy partygoers, real people with real drinks, real canapés, real frocks, and real jokes. The crowd was lit romantically by lanterns that bedecked the garden the of the Gousset's home. The house itself, a backdrop of scaffolding and tarps, like a set for an epic film under construction, was being rebuilt even as the revelry progressed. Tables beneath the topiary were laden with multiple banquets, staff circulated with more drinks, a small orchestra played waltzes and underground art-rock hits by turns.

Many of the human partygoers were slightly less sentient than the topiary but definitely more loquacious. There were heads of state, celebrities, dignitaries, nobility, and pretty well everybody involved in the rescue of Victoria from Alamut, whether they had been of any actual use or not (invariably not).

This was Hades' big celebration for getting his daughter back, uneaten and in one healthy piece, albeit with attractively altered hair colour.

'Oh, Timmy, there you are!'

'Hello, Victoria. How are you?'

'Obviously, I'm fine. The question is how are you? You really have been through the wars.'

'I'm fairly blue, thank you, Victoria.'

'Oh, cheer up! Everything's pretty well sorted. We're on terra firma. No harm done. And we have this big party to enjoy.'

'No, I mean I'm somewhat the colour blue. Although the doctors managed to thaw me out after being in the snowdrift, they couldn't get rid of the frozen blue colour I'd picked up.'

'Oh, I see. That would explain your blue hue now.'

'Yes, it would. Look, I'm sorry I failed to save you at Villa Parque, and I'm sorry I kidnapped you at Disneyland. Stealing you seemed like the best chance for us to be alone together so that I could express my true feelings for you.'

'But we were alone together lots before that. You were my personal assistant. We were alone at Villa Parque.'

Timmy palmed his forehead. 'Fish tails! So we were! Why didn't I think of saying something then?'

'You just need some practice thinking of things. You'll get there in the end. Meanwhile, I don't blame you at all for Villa Parque or Disneyland. We all learned something and we all came out unscathed. You still have a job at Pants Corp if you want it. Think on it and we'll talk later.'

'Thank you, Victoria.'

'What's that funny smell? Timmy, come on, I think Seamus is here.'

Seamus was indeed there, hiding among some of the bigger bushes. Whether he was more embarrassed about being found smoking a joint or wearing the immaculate dinner jacket, wasn't clear.

'You managed to drag yourself away from Alamut? I didn't think you ever would.'

'Ah, well, you see, it was getting a bit busy there. Not

what it was.'

'And the Iranian government had opinions about a bunch of potheads squatting a national heritage site, as it turned out,' put in Billy over Seamus's shoulder.

'Imagine that! I heard that Daddy had invited you to the party. That was big of him. And big of you to come.'

'Oh, I dunno. Free munchies — who's going to say no?'

'So what are you doing with yourself other than lurking in the bushes?'

Seamus looked hunted. 'Nothing as usual. Keeping it real.'

'Yeah, really real,' chirped Billy in obvious delight. 'Seamus got a job!'

'Shut up, Billy. I did not *get* a job.'

'True enough, you maybe didn't go out and *get* the job, but you were given one, no doubt about that!'

'I said shut up Billy or I'll bogart this whole doobie without letting you have any. I just let them think I was going to have a job.'

'What's this about a job? Really, Seamus? Is this a new way to bring the world to its sofa?'

Seamus snarled like a cornered rat. 'Drop it, OK?'

Billy was high on the moment not to mention other things and took no notice. 'Yeah, his da' contracts for your da' and so his da' had a word with your da' and your da' gave him a job.'

'You're working for Pants Corp? That's hil— that's splendid! What on earth are you doing for Hades?'

Seamus wasn't sure he was more put out for being discovered to have a job or by the tone of Victoria's voice that suggested he wasn't able to do one, and simply skulked.

Billy continued to help out. 'He's going to be an underpants tester. What do you think of that?'

Victoria was incredulous. 'What? Like those brave test pilots in Dad's experimental lab?'

'Nah, not a bit of it! He'll be testing the regular pants for leaks. "We need an incontinent bastard like that in our research department," is what your da' said.'

'Billy, I warned you!' Seamus sucked furiously on his joint in Billy's face, telling Billy he wasn't getting any. Billy happily waved his own doobie in the face of his wannabe tormentor.

'Well, that's splendid news,' said Colonel Kim Il-bond cramming himself into the already crowded bush space with Victoria, Timmy, Seamus and Billy. 'Finally doing something productive. Your brief brush with the supreme ethic of self-denial and unceasing work of Our Supremely Kissable Leader has inspired you, and left you with a new self-sacrificing outlook on life.'

Kim took a huge bite of a massive ice-cream-topped sticky bun and washed it down with a swig from a brandy snifter the size of a bucket.

'Erm,' said Victoria, Seamus and Billy together.

'I too have a new job,' said the colonel, cream piling up on the end of his nose.

'You've been promoted in the Pyongyang party hierarchy,' guessed Victoria.

'Not at all,' said Kim, cramming more into his face. 'I have made a lateral move, as it were. I have left the party hierarchy and opened a Korean restaurant in Soho. I have employed the whole team. Your father graciously fronted the capital.'

Victoria thought this was a great move up from flying around in an airborne jalopy looking for treats for the dear leader. 'That's fantastic! How's it going? Do you have a lot of customers?'

'Not yet. There's a small glitch in the operation. Very little of the food makes it from the kitchen to the table of the diners. It's an issue we are working on.'

'Well, if you get it fixed, let me know and I'll come round with some friends. Something fab has come out of this whole convoluted misadventure, after all.'

The sky exploded with colour and noise. Fireworks threw the remains of the family mansion into vivid silhouette, the music crescendoed and Hades ascended the main stage, his image repeated on projection screens around the garden.

'Ladies and gentlemen! So glad you could all come. I am deeply grateful and indebted —'

'Oh,' said Victoria. 'My father is making a speech. I'm supposed to be up there with him.' She sighed.

'I can tell by your face you don't want to be part of that. Let's grab a bottle and all of us hide a bit deeper in these bushes. What do you say?' Seamus was flushed with unbecoming enthusiasm for an indolent young man.

'Hold that thought, Seamus. Keep a bottle for me. My parents may be mad as bats, and they may have mislaid me, but the main thing is, I'm back home at last.'

Also by Chris Page

The Underpants Tree

Whoever controls underwear controls the world!

The Underpants Tree is the sequel to King of the Undies World.

Sir Hades Gousset — underwear magnate, king of the undies world, the biggest man in pants — has only ever seen underwear as a force for good. That is, until the mysterious Dr Hieronymus Mangler appears with a fiendish new technology that threatens Hades' monopoly and his grip on the world of nether-wear.

Mangler's technology has more sinister purposes than business competition and his ambitions go beyond mere financial profit. The battle between Hades and Mangler for control of this vital undergarment becomes a titanic struggle for the soul of humanity itself, and leads to not just one, but two apocalypses, in a conflict that rocks civilisation to its foundation wear.

"Thank-you for making my days funnier and reminding me that laughter really is the best medicine. Loved the book!"
— Anna Yamato, writing on Facebook

Weed

In his professional and personal life Bob, aka Robert D Weed, is deemed totally useless — or, perhaps, he is the smart one and everyone around him is terminally daft.

Bob is a human weed who is tugged and pulled by a world that wants to uproot him but which discovers that he cannot be so easily tossed on the compost.

"... it's really witty and very strong ... I would compare the writing to Robert Rankin, or a really satirically biting Tom Sharpe, and will say [...] that I'm really impressed by it." — A London publisher

"... Weed ... is a tale that somehow manages to combine the frustrations of modern urban Mclife and blancmange abuse in the same story... a tale that is likely to feel sheepishly familiar yet feverishly alien... depending on your views about the uses of sticky puddings." — Kyoto After Dark

"Weed is a brilliantly written comedic novel while at the same time a harsh criticism of modern consumerist society. The lyrically attractive writing style spoke to me and does a good job of creating a vision of this fictitious yet very real world and company. It reminded me of Terry Gilliam's movie Brazil ... If you, like the protagonist, sometimes find yourself drowning in the rat race for conformity and mediocrity, this book is for you." — Amazon review

"It's so funny I Weed myself. Geddit?" — The author made up this quote himself.

Sanctioned

Are you dead weight?

Britain is sinking under the weight of scroungers, skivers, shirkers, refugees, migrants, libtards and experts. The economy is hobbled and the very fabric of society is in need of a good scrubbing. Gideon Smith, an agent of the Department of Aspiration, has been tasked with doing something about it — and in no uncertain terms.

Another Perfect Day in Fucking Paradise

Ben seems to be the only living person on the planet and the dead are really getting on his nerves.

But then he discovers he may not be alone.

Can Ben find love among the dead or will death find him first?

Another Perfect Day in Fucking Paradise is the fifth novel (or first novella) from Chris Page and is a blend of high farce and low horror.

Un-Tall Tales

Un-Tall Tales is a collection of short fiction, poetry, flash fiction and odds and ends.

In 'The Freebie', musical wannabe Billy Freeb's fifteen minutes are upon him. Will he survive?

The poems explore underpants, teeth, chickens, and tombstones. Will literary sensibility survive?

'Cats Die' relates how our hero decides to combat the crisis of middle age by having an affair with a teenage girl. Will he survive?

The hero of 'Dumb Novel' achieves literary fame for a book he didn't write. Will he survive?

'Escapology' — on a whim, the hero has himself chained, locked in a box and dropped through a hole drilled in the Arctic ice cap. Will he survive?

'Bog' is a bloggy rumination on sausages and twigs. Will the human attention span survive?

Before you go …

Find out more on these sites:
chris-page.com
psipook.com
weedthenovel.com

And finally — please support your local struggling artist (without spending any more money)

If you've read and enjoyed a book by Chris Page, please consider giving it a star rating and/or review on Amazon and/or Goodreads. These ratings really do help. They raise the title in the rankings and reassure potential readers that the story is not actually toxic or liable to cause injury.

The author thanks you in advance.

www.ingramcontent.com/pod-product-compliance
Lightning Source LLC
Chambersburg PA
CBHW071450040426
42444CB00008B/1277